IT STARTS WITH ME

An Anthology Of The Magic That Happens When Women Reclaim Their
Strength & Their Stories

DANI WALLACE

NICKI JAMES

authors
AND CO.

DEDICATION

For Betty and Rene.

We pay our strengths forward just as you did.

We are part of your legacy.

You are part of ours.

CONTENTS

INTRODUCTION

Nicki James and Dani Wallace first started working together at the beginning of 2020.

When they met in the online entrepreneurial space mid-2019, Nicki, a champion of women and a leading light in the brand industry and Dani, one of the most exciting motivational public speakers and speaking coaches in the UK, it truly was a meeting of minds and hearts.

Both of them had chaotic and difficult formative years. Their stories could have taken them in wildly different and much less positive directions, as it does for many, but they each created lives and businesses that now help thousands of people the world over.

Both have gone on to create incredible success for themselves in a space where, for their audiences, authenticity, truth, and absolutely owning who they are has been THE key ingredient to their rise.

In both of their businesses, Nicki with Just Brand You and Dani with the 'I Am The Queen Bee' Movement, work with business owners to show up in their truth, so they become magnetic for their perfect audiences.

Nicki, a gifted designer, having worked on, and for national and global campaigns and companies, knew there was more to branding than mere design.

After many years in brand design work, Nicki knew that a brand is much more than a pretty logo and website. She knew that the people and stories at the very centre of a brand are what makes a brand compelling and magnetic. She has made it her mission to build her business, Just Brand You and The I.AM.ME Collective, in service of entrepreneurs, companies and public figures who are ready to stop hiding and to connect much more deeply with their purpose.

Nicki works with business owners to define, become and live their brands. She helps people both in the UK and internationally, uncover their true brand story and mission. She then translates that into showstopping assets and visuals and then sets them up for success with her razor-sharp strategy and business expertise.

With over 20 years experience on the stage and having worked at the top level in leadership and training for several well known global brands, Dani works with entrepreneurs, celebrities and charities to help them speak their business and mission messages so that they reach more people and make more sales both on and off stage. From media preparation to TEDx talks, Dani is fast becoming the go-to girl for all things articulation.

Dani is an expert in the field of personal and business development as well as that of speech and stagecraft, and this makes for a winning combination when it comes to raising a businesses profile, positioning and authority.

When a queen meets a fellow queen to discuss their mutual slay, magic occurs, and that is exactly what happened when Nicki and Dani decided to bring together their powerhouse expertise for a project that would prove to be life-changing for all involved.

Together, they created their business mastermind programme, The Rock Star Level Up to help entrepreneurs who were ready to turn the dial up on their brand from the inside out and step up into the levels of success and visibility their businesses deserve.

Each bringing to the table their combined arsenal of awesome, Nicki and Dani have worked with some of the brightest, breakthrough businesses in the UK as part of the mastermind and this anthology has been created in celebration of them and their stories.

Each of the chapters in this book are written by members of the 2020 cohort of the Rockstar Level Up.

Every contributor whose story you read has embraced where they have come from and, in turn, are fully focussed on where they are going. They know that their success starts with them.

Allowing themselves to be visible in ways they never thought possible, the women in this book are beacons of light for their industries and for the people they serve.

Just as Dani and Nicki both harnessed the power of their stories to create incredible lives and businesses, so the legacy continues with new waves of talented, brave, strong women turning up the dial, allowing themselves to be heard and taking up their rightful space in the business world.

Nicki and Dani continue their work into 2021 and beyond, creating the ripples that turn in to waves that turn into tsunamis of women in business rising up.

It started with them.

It started with the phenomenal contributors to this book.

Now it starts with YOU.

If you want to know more about the Rockstar Level up and how you can get involved, go follow Nicki and Dani on social media right now and let's turn the dial up together!

———

Nicki James Social Media

Instagram @JustBrandYou

Facebook @JustBrandYou

———

Dani Wallace Social Media

Instagram @TheQueenBeeDani

Facebook @TheQueenBeeDani

1

ALISON BOOTE

WHY GET UNCOMFORTABLE?

Me. Doing a mastermind? Writing a book? Going LIVE on social media?

These are not the sort of things I thought I'd ever find myself doing. These things 'weren't for me'. They were for everyone else. I just did the 'safe' stuff. I got along with everything quietly in the background. Doing well. Doing 'enough'. But not as well as I really knew I was capable of. Not as much as I knew was in me.

I just did what was *comfortable*.

I mean, if you can get along in life and do ok by playing it safe then why bother putting yourself out there? We all want an easy life so why make things any more difficult for yourself if you really don't have to?

Well, maybe we just get to that point where we know we are destined for bigger things. We know we have more to give. To others. To ourselves.

I worked with a client recently on her branding. She was my first client to go through my new system and processes that I'd worked hard at putting into place. I put everything into the job like I do with any work I do. I always have done, from when I worked at various design agencies, since I've been freelance, and now being self-employed. I delivered the job as if she was a client paying £10k to a full service design agency.

And I charged a few hundred quid for it.

When we finished the job and I handed everything over to her she was blown away and couldn't believe what I'd delivered. Along with telling me that my pricing did not reflect the quality of my work she told me I was her "best kept secret".

Best kept secret.

I learnt a lot from that:

I'm very good at what I do.

I over-deliver.

I should believe in myself more.

And I should be charging more.

As a brand designer I help others stand out for what they're so great at. But I'd not really been doing this for myself. I didn't want to be a secret anymore though. I had always just got on with things quietly, but I got to the point where I knew if I was serious about running my own business then now was the time I needed to really do something about it and stop playing safe.

I needed to get out of my comfort zone...

SCHOOL AND UNIVERSITY

I always did well at school. Like, really well. I was in the top class for everything. The captain of every sports team. And I didn't really need to try that hard. I mean I applied myself, yes, but most things just seemed to come naturally to me. I was talented in many things, but I never really made the most out of these skills. I never pushed myself.

I was selected to play hockey for the county in my teens. I bloody loved hockey, and this was amazing. There was me and one other girl from my school who were selected for the county team. She was a goalkeeper, so it was just me out on the field where everyone else knew each other. I didn't really enjoy it because of this. So I never pursued it because it made me feel uncomfortable.

Comfort. The safety of being in my comfort zone seems to have been a running theme. I was good enough at things so did I really need to push any further? I got top grades, I did well, so why get uncomfortable?

It followed me to university. Going to uni in itself was a little step out of the comfort zone but I knew I needed to go to follow my plan of becoming a graphic designer. New places. New people. I got the grades to go to any uni I had wanted really. But I stayed close to home. It made sense. Staffordshire University was considered a great uni for design and my design teacher told me not to disregard it because it was close by. So, I lived at home and drove there each day, leaving at night to go back home - where it was familiar.

Again, at uni I did well. I graduated with a first, but I didn't make the most of my time there. There were lots of things I could have explored - extra courses and work-shops - things I could have used to improve my projects. Photography, screen printing, woodwork... nah, I'll just stick to what I know, it's going well like that. Why get uncomfortable?

When I think back to the things I could have achieved if I'd pushed out of my comfort zone it makes me a bit sad about the opportunities I may have missed and the experi-ences I could have had. If I could go back and give myself some of the confidence I now have, who knows what I could have done.

WORK EXPERIENCE

At the end of uni we put on a show in London for D&AD - it's the place to be seen for new creatives. Off the back of that I was offered work experience at a top branding agency in Leeds. It was a bit far from home, but I couldn't let that opportunity pass. Competition was strong for graphic design jobs and even for work experience, particularly at a top agency like this one. I had to do it.

A school friend offered me a place to stay at his house in Manchester where he was sharing with some others. Perfect - that cut the journey down by half. So, the first morning I got up, got ready and set off. I wasn't used to driving around cities by myself (I grew up at the very edge of a town close to the countryside) so I got lost around the M60, went all over the place and then managed to head off in the direction of Leeds. I decided it would be much easier to go back home that evening and just travel all the way there each day using the way I know. Two and a half hours commute each way every day in the height of summer, with no air conditioning in my little car, was nothing was it really? ... I mean, the alternative was doing something out of my comfort zone and finding my way round unfamiliar roads.

I didn't really make the most of my time there either. It was such a big change for me being in one of the UK's top design agencies, that I suppose I felt completely out of place. I wasn't at all confident in my talent and felt like everyone there was so much better than me. But I was so quietly excited inside to be working alongside top creatives, working on projects for huge well-known brands and just being in that environment. It was what I wanted but my comfort zone was calling and enticing me back in with no commute and people and places I was familiar with.

Needless to say, I didn't pursue employment there and left on my last day with a quiet 'thank you very much' and added it to my CV to help me get other work experience. Looking back, that was my dream job. And I was lucky enough, or should I say, talented enough to be approached by *them* for me to go and spend time with them on a work placement. But I mean, leave home, relocate, meet new people, find my way round somewhere new… woooahhhh that might mean getting uncomfortable, right?

If I'd had some of the confidence then that I have now, things could have been very different. I probably walked away from some amazing opportunities. That particular agency had offices all over the world and staff quite often transferred from one to another. Thinking about those things did always make me feel excited about the possibilities but I always seemed to bring myself back down and be thinking, "that's not for *you* though, Alison." Playing it safe often leaves us missing out on some amazing things.

GETTING A JOB

I went for an interview at a top agency in Manchester. It was huge, with departments for photography, account management, admin, artwork and design. It was one of those cool looking places with exposed brick, funky light fittings and a wall covered in framed past work for recognisable and high-profile brands. This was where I needed to be.

My interview went amazingly well and one of the owners who interviewed me was so impressed with my portfolio he called for the Creative Director to come down to us. They wanted to know where my typographical knowledge had come from and what my background was... well, my Mum's a Sample Machinist and my Dad's a Welder....

"I don't know where we're going to put you, but we'll find somewhere."

So, I got my first job as a Junior Designer and was put on a pod of desks with the Senior Designers. This was much to the annoyance of a couple of them as it seemed this wasn't the 'done' thing. I 'should have' started off in the artwork department and then worked my way up into design (apparently).

I loved being there and working with the kinds of clients I was working with. I learnt so much and was starting to become more confident generally - being myself and believing in my abilities. The hour-long commute each way was starting to become a little tiring and I knew I needed to make a decision to move closer or find a job closer to home. So I left, having been offered an opportunity closer to home. I could have moved to Manchester or at least a bit closer and kept my dream job, but that would mean getting uncomfortable and you must be starting to see now how I felt about that…

When I look back, this could have been another amazing opportunity I threw away to get back into my comfort zone. We don't see things like this at the time. I think we make excuses in our own minds about why the comfortable route is the one to take. Maybe it's our subconscious way of keeping ourselves 'safe'. I don't know.

GETTING A MORE COMFORTABLE JOB

My next job was at a lovely small family-run agency in the next town. I was back living at home - back where it was familiar. And familiar equates to me feeling comfortable. Being part of a small team I naturally took on lots of responsibility and was a key team member. I really loved it there and had worked my way up to being a midweight designer. The work was really varied and I loved the people I worked with. I really felt I'd found the perfect job.

As much as I did really love it there, looking back I know I had walked away from a dream job for the second time.

MET A BOY

During this time, I met a boy. Well I was 23, so he wasn't really a boy. But I met Joe. He was very different from me. He lived for the moment, would give anything a try and believed that anything was possible. We'd been together around twelve months when he suggested we go travelling. A full round the world job. Part of me was full of excitement at the thought of doing that - seeing the world, having new experiences, breaking away from the ties of a 9-5. (And it was just the done thing back then.)

But how could *I* possibly do that? The girl who wouldn't move an hour away to keep her dream job...

But we went. We started in America and moved on to Fiji, New Zealand, Australia, Singapore and finally Thailand. We were away for around four months and had an amazing time. I had so many new experiences and I started to learn that anything IS possible. You just find a way. But you've got to push yourself and go out there and find things. Amazing things and experiences don't just come knocking on the door of your comfort zone.

BACK FROM THE WORLD

We returned home in December. It was a bit of a shock coming back from Thailand, where it was beyond hot, to England where it was snowing and dark and very dreary. Back to life. Back to reality. There didn't seem any other option except to go and get a 9-5 again. Travelling felt like it had just been a dream. An escape from the ties of daily routines.

My employers had left the door open for me but unfortunately things had gone a bit quiet and they no longer had enough work on to take me back. So, I set about finding a new job. I got one at a medium sized agency not too far away. I hated it. It was one of those jobs that gave you the Sunday night feeling of dread, knowing you'd be off there again the next day. It just wasn't for me.

Twelve months later, my previous employer got back in touch with me and I went back to work for them. I was so happy to go back to an agency I loved working for and people I loved working with. I went on to spend a long time at that agency and I learnt a lot. I progressed to being a Senior Designer and was working on some great stuff. But I started to get a bit frustrated after being there so long. I started to feel a bit restricted as I felt I had better ways of doing things, better ways of working and I started to want to do things MY way. It was only a small agency and I had begun to reach the ceiling for the amount they were going to be able to pay me.

I was starting to get fed up of being comfortable. I didn't feel like I was challenging myself and I wanted more for myself.

SELF-EMPLOYMENT

I married that boy I went round the world with, and we started to think about having a family of our own. But I couldn't see how that was going to fit in with working at an agency 9-5. I think travelling had given me a taste of setting my own agenda and not answering to anybody else. So, with flexibility and earning potential in mind I made the decision to step away from full time employment and become self-employed and I became a freelance designer.

This was a huge step for me. I had so much knowledge and I'd had lots of experience of managing projects and dealing with clients that it seemed like a natural progression. A higher earning potential and being able to do things my way and say no when I wanted to was a big draw. It felt a bit scary to make the decision, but it felt like the next logical step.

This was the start of me finally getting away from being in that cosy little comfort zone. It was a huge step for me, but

I wouldn't be where I am today if I hadn't been brave enough to do it.

When I took the decision to go freelance my employers didn't really want me to go. So they kept me busy with freelance work. I did most of it by going in and working there as well as some bits at home. I loved it. I had a nice balance of being part of a team and working in an agency but I also had the option to say no. My goals of greater freedom and flexibility and the ability to earn more were being met.

I had a number of other clients that I did work for - most of whom I had worked with previously either on a free-lance basis or in another capacity, and they all came back to me for further work. So the freelance world was working out great for me. Nice and comfortable you might say…

INCOMING BABIES

Just over a year after becoming freelance we had our first baby, Ruby. I loved becoming a mum and having the flexi-bility of not being tied to a 9-5 was perfect. I then fell back into working freelance for my old employer on a regular basis and after a while I became a part time employee for them again which, at the time, suited us both. I felt I needed that security of regular income and a routine of working set days whilst still not working full weeks whilst I was still navigating my way through parenthood.

But I ended up feeling like I'd taken a step backwards and had that frustration of wanting to work to my own schedule, do things my own way and be able to say no. It reinforced my feelings that I had to push myself to do something that was mine, on my terms. So, I became freelance again.

Back in my own business again I spent a lot of time suffering from what I now know as "Shiny Object Syndrome". I was doing all the things in terms of my offering and I was also doing all the things in terms of marketing. I had the luxury of freelance work bringing in enough income for it not to matter that all this messing around I was doing didn't make an impact on my earnings. It was keeping me in my comfort zone as I didn't do anything that I didn't want to do. And I didn't really need to. I was earning good money, why get uncomfortable?

A few years later baby number two was due and the freelance work had started to slow down from my old employer. I knew I needed to build up my own business in order to carry me through and replace the regular salary I had been used to. So, I decided I needed to sort myself out, stop messing around and really make a go of things.

I scrapped a lot of what I was doing and focused on what I had always done and always loved - branding.

THINGS STARTED TO CHANGE

Knowing I had another baby on the way and that I had to make my business work to replace my previous income pushed me into action and things started to change. I started taking little steps out of my comfort zone. I decided to focus my branding on helping other mums like me, who started their own businesses when starting a family, for the many reasons that we do - flexibility, freedom, solving a problem they had encountered in pregnancy or parenthood, a better work/life balance, doing something for themselves (the list goes on…).

This meant sharing my story in order to connect with my audience. I never liked sharing anything on social media and would usually question the motives of others who did. But I started to post. I started to share more about me and my journey. I talked about what I did and how it could help them. I even went LIVE! The first time I did a live video, simply introducing myself, I thought my heart was going to jump out of my chest. I said 'erm' after, erm, every, erm, word. And I developed some kind of weird swallow. I also hated the sound of my own voice.

Things were starting to go well but the strain of the pregnancy was taking its toll. I had a back issue which was causing me incredible pain, Ruby needed my attention, and I had the added stress that only twelve months after

Joe's mum had passed away, my Dad was diagnosed with terminal cancer. I had to stop.

I took some time away from the business to concentrate on just getting through life and along came Ollie. During that time I did a lot of learning. I learnt a lot about mindset and the blocks we often put in place. I realised that I was a perfectionist and that it was really holding me back. I had such high standards that I often wouldn't start something or implement something because I would worry it wouldn't be good enough. I had always been the best at everything I did but this world of business was new to me and I had a lot to learn.

I learnt that perfectionism very often leads to overwhelm and procrastination. And these were the things that had been holding me back. So, whilst taking time away from the business I did a lot of work on my mindset. Reading up on it and listening to podcasts, I started to see patterns in the way I'd do (or not do) things. Ways and reasons I'd stay in my comfort zone.

BACK FROM MATERNITY, AGAIN

As I did with Ruby, I got Ollie into nursery early on for three days a week. I got back to starting to build my business. I started to network online. This was not something that came at all naturally to me in the beginning, but I knew I needed to do it in order to get my business seen and find clients. I joined a couple of online business memberships. I somehow thought that just being in them and lurking in the background would help me move forwards... it didn't. Eventually I started to get involved a bit more. I put myself forward to do a live in one group membership to talk about branding to help others. And I survived. I actually really enjoyed it.

I then went crazy and went to an in-person meet-up from one of the memberships. By myself. BY MYSELF. This may not seem like much to some people but this was *huge* for me. This was not the kind of thing you would find me doing but I knew that I had to. My Dad had passed away, I was still getting used to trying to keep some kind of control over a baby and a pre-schooler at the same time, as well as dealing with the immense nerve pain my back was causing. I really didn't feel like myself. I could easily have stayed back in the good old comfort zone but where was it going to get me? Nowhere fast.

AND NOW

I went to that meet-up and that is where I got my client who ended up telling me I was her "best kept secret". This was a bit of a wakeup call. Part of me saw this as a compliment that she obviously saw the skills I had. But another part of me was annoyed with myself that I wasn't doing more to get out there and show more people what I'm capable of and make myself known.

If I'm so good at something why am I hiding myself away? I had started to step out of my comfort zone but I had to do it more.

Getting uncomfortable has led me to start sharing more about me and my business. It's led me to go LIVE. It's led me to invest in myself and push myself - masterminds, coaching, mindset work. And what has that led to? Paying clients. And a business that continues to grow.

It's led me to see what others have seen in me all along. I've got a talent and I'm going to make the most of it. I've got a wealth of experience in branding, design and print and I'm going to make sure I use that to help others push themselves so they can make their mark in the world and do what they do best - not just float along in the background like I had been doing.

I feel like I've wasted a lot of time and missed a lot of opportunities by staying in my comfort zone.

SO, WHY GET UNCOMFORTABLE?

Because that's where the good stuff happens.

I'm determined to keep taking steps out of my comfort zone to keep pushing myself and I am definitely a work in progress. I don't want to miss out on opportunities anymore by holding back. I'm fed up of watching others, often with less skill and experience than I have, doing well just because they're brave enough to step out of their comfort zones, push forwards and just do the things they need to.

It's important to remember that everyone's comfort zones look different but if we stop and actually think about the things we aren't doing and why we aren't doing them we'll see that we often hold ourselves back. We get in our own way.

So if you don't want to let those amazing opportunities pass you by then try taking little steps out of that comfort zone – it may not be as bad as you think. And you'll thank yourself later down the line that you started with even the littlest of steps.

ABOUT THE AUTHOR

Alison Boote

Alison Boote is a brand expert who helps super skilled people push their businesses to the next level.

She is passionate about helping people and their businesses really shine for what they're best at. She is a self-confessed over-deliverer and recovering perfectionist who now uses these things to her advantage to work at a high level helping others with their branding and design.

Alison has a thirteen-year design career behind her. During this time she has worked with brands of all sizes, from local startups to luxury global brands. She has worked for clients in a whole range of industries, from Dutch barges and vodka bars, luxury blinds and restaurant chains to offshore energy, Italian pasta and everything in between.

Alison now draws upon this wealth of experience to help small businesses, using branding, design and print to help them look the part, make their mark and stand out for what they're best at.

CONTACT

EMAIL: alison@alisonboote.com

WEBSITE: www.alisonboote.com

 facebook.com/alisonbootebrandstudio

 instagram.com/alisonbootebrandstudio

2

AMANDA HUTCHINSON

Brave or Crazy? Either way - I'm free!

It was the 13th March 2019, and I sat across the table from my manager, heart pounding, ready to take the biggest jump of my life (and I've sky dived!) – to take back some control in my life and to be honest, I felt sick to the stomach.

All those fears and doubts came rushing to my head, the 'what-ifs' and the imposter syndrome, but I knew I had to do it. I had to at least try.

So, I uttered the words... I'm handing in my notice.

You see, I'd been working in crisis management for twelve years, a solid career, I was really good at my job and it paid reasonably well. It was as secure as a job these days could be and let's face it, 2020 has certainly shown us there will always be a crisis to plan and respond to. It just wasn't for me anymore; the buzz didn't fire me up and it was time to call it a day.

But what brought me to this point, the point of "throwing away a career" (as one colleague said to me when the news broke)? I'm going to take you back on a bit of a journey, to show that wherever life starts, the twists and turns keep you on your toes…

A NOMADIC CHILDHOOD

Growing up as a child we moved around a lot as a family: being in the military does that. It never ceases to amaze me the number of people who say, "Oh that must have been so hard," and don't get me wrong, like any kid, there are times at school that aren't exactly rainbows and unicorns. You get bullies wherever you go, but at least with moving so much I was able leave them behind and on to the next adventure.

See, for me, the moving and the change was exciting, and to be honest I didn't know any different. Having moved house a few times as an adult, I now know how stressful it was for my parents always moving us and packing up, but my Mum has unpacking a house down to a fine art, always starting with the kettle! To be honest, the idea of being in one place gives me itchy feet. I wonder if I'll ever end up with a "forever home". It's those itchy feet that probably explains the career path I chose, how I came to be in the career I did.

Anyway, I digress... The thing about being a military child is that you build a lot of resilience, and as we got older, we began to understand the risks involved for my Dad when he went away. You learn to adapt, to be able to put on a brave face and to be there for those around you when things feel like they are crumbling, and in turn, I learnt the true value of friendship and who would really be there for you when the chips were down.

That resilience saw me go through four primary schools, two secondary schools and on to University, where I met the friends who cemented what true friendship meant, along with my now husband, the biggest support and champion I have, that led me to be sitting in that meeting room, handing in my notice.

It was at Uni, where I went from studying Psychology to volunteering in South Africa that I was drawn back to this word "resilience", not just as a personal construct but as a career path and so I went back and studied for my MSc in Disaster Management, in turn, paving my way into the world of Crisis Management − a true roller coaster of a career!

LIFE ON CALL – NEVER A DULL MOMENT

Emergency Planning – a team in every Council across the UK whose job it is to plan for and respond to any emergency or crisis that is thrown at its residents. And here started the thrill of working in this field. I was thrown into the middle of a huge emergency in my first week, fresh from Uni and straight into rolling up my sleeves helping coordinate the response and protection of staff after a harrowing child protection case.

From there on in, it was a constant cycle of being on call, so that there was always a Council response alongside the Police, Fire and Ambulance services. From burst water mains, bomb threats, gas leaks, fires and culminating in the London riots in 2011, it was busy but the thrill and adrenaline is what I think keeps so many people going, working in that field.

However, in the "down time" I was able to pursue another avenue to make a difference – building resilience within the wider Council team and our communities. I was helping put plans and provisions in place for a whole raft of scenarios, something I later realised I did in my own life, always seeing what "could go wrong". This way of thinking has required some serious taming further down the line.

But ultimately, working in local government comes with a lot of red tape and hurdles, something that became increasingly frustrating and started to sap the enjoyment from the job. I still got the buzz from an incident, but I was starting to feel like I had no control over my time and my life. Being on call meant that plans would have to go on hold, I was restricted to staying local-ish to the borough, and that never knowing when something would happen feeling, the feeling that I used to thrive on, which started materialising into anxiety and spilling into all areas of my life.

Whilst planning for the biggest live exercise of my life – a scenario role played by nearly 300 characters to rehearse the response to a major incident with multiple casualties and fatalities – to identify where improvements could be made as part of the gear up for the Olympics, I was presented with the opportunity to take this hands-on experience into the corporate world.

And so, after months of planning, logistics and script writing, the exercise was complete, in just over half a day (a bit like Christmas dinner, it takes so much preparation and it's devoured in no time!), and I realised I'd achieved what I wanted to; there was nowhere else for me to go . So, I seized the opportunity for a new adventure with nervous but excited hands, and handed in my notice for the first time in my career… leaving my bubble of five years to head to the City!

LIKE ALICE THROUGH THE LOOKING GLASS

I think changing sector or industry in any job is a big adjustment, but to go from local authority to corporate life, I felt like Alice stepping through the looking glass. It was a completely different world – for starters it involved a whole new wardrobe – you can't turn up to an emergency in a pencil skirt and high heels. My attire had always been "response chic", not quite what this role would need.

But that personal resilience kicked in again. Starting a new job is like starting a new school: there are the same ready-made groups to navigate, the same office/playground politics and a new way of working to get your head around.

I felt again like I had some semblance of control over my life. I didn't have to wait with bated breath to see if the phone would go off. My evenings and weekends were my own again! This gave me more of an opportunity to pursue my photography, a passion that was already growing as a bit of a side business.

My ex-local authority colleagues thought I'd miss the thrill and adrenaline rush. To be honest, I do a bit. Even now when something happens my pulse quickens. I feel like I need to jump into action and that I should be there, helping, being part of that response. After a while, it felt refreshing that I wasn't always on edge, waiting for something to happen and the new role gave me plenty of new challenges. Travel was exciting and I got to work with a whole range of global businesses and brands, from food and spirits manufacturers, to fashion brands and household names. What was second nature to me, being able to respond in a crisis, I was needing to translate into how a business could bounce back and survive – I was spreading the resilience I'd grown.

However, after a few years, that itchy feet feeling came creeping back, this time with the frustration that I was sitting on the side lines of some pretty big incidents happening in London. I felt overworked, underappreciated and unfulfilled, all tied up in this lack of control I had over my own life as the client work stacked up and the travel became extensive. I think I spent more time on trains than I did with clients or in the office.

That lacking a sense of achievement and balance left me unsettled, but the fear of the unknown, of what I do next was paralysing. I was going to be stuck in the corporate world for the rest of my working life.

My photography gave me a creative outlet. I loved being able to work with couples and businesses to create the images they really wanted. But the more anxious I got at work, the more I needed the photography to balance that out. The more pressure I felt at work, the more I needed the photography as an outlet for the increasing anxiety.

A string of occurrences that took place in 2018 both personally and to those around me started the questions bubbling in my head, "how do I get out?" The feeling of dread had reached the point where I'd stand outside the office for a good ten to fifteen minutes, just trying to summon up the strength to walk in, to face another day. And don't get me wrong, I loved the people I worked with (well most of them), it really was a case of "it's not you, it's me". The environment didn't help dampen down this need to escape and that was making me miserable and on edge, but not in the productive, spring into action in an emergency way that I'd become accustomed to in previous years. But that fear of the unknown was sapping my confidence…

FROM CRISIS TO CONFIDENCE

There's a surprising correlation between crisis management and camera confidence, but it's only looking back and doing a lot of soul searching that this realisation has hit me, so bear with me!

The fear or thrill of the unknown that I had thrived on for so long eventually became unsettling and a feeling of no control. But this actually led to a real lack in confidence in all aspects of my life. It had spread through me like one of those quick growing plants you can never get rid of. (Gardening is not my strong point so I've no idea what it's called!)

But throughout my career I actually witnessed this all the time: CEOs and high-flying executives of big businesses unsure of what to do and how to respond to media scrutiny – not knowing what to do or say, but once they had a plan in place and some guidance, they were confident – that fear was dispelled. And I see it so much in everyday life, within myself and others around me.

- That timid feeling of entering a room full of people
- Not going for what you want because you don't believe it'll work
- Avoiding the camera / going live on social media because you don't know what to do or say or what people will think

We're taught to get comfortable with that fear, that it's protecting us, telling us not to rock the status quo. And it does protect us to a certain extent, it makes us assess risk. But it holds us back, and stops us from thriving, at least that's what it was doing to me and I don't think I'm alone in this one.

I didn't want to work for someone else, to do a job for the next however many years where I didn't love it. To stand in front of the building with dread in my belly, thinking, "Oh jeez, here we go again."

So, there I sat…

… After 7 years in that job, being really good at what I did… handing my notice in. Ready to take the leap, to take some time back for me, to build the photography business to what I felt it could be, no, scrap that, knew it could be, even though the prospect terrified me.

In the days that followed my friends and colleagues at work fell into two camps:

- You're so brave!
- You're mad!

It was hard for some people, so passionate about their area in risk, so ingrained in the corporate world (which there's nothing wrong with, it just wasn't for me!) to understand why I would want to leave the safety of a "9-5 job" that paid well and had security, to well, no job. It probably didn't help that I got so fed up of the question about what I was going to do next, that I said I was leaving to learn to draw and to speak French – neither of them I have done, mind you!

But life is too short to do something you are starting to hate. I knew if I stuck it out then it would eventually turn to resentment, my confidence would be rock bottom and ultimately that wasn't fair on me, my colleagues or the clients we worked with.

There were certainly moments when I thought what the hell had I done, but I learnt that by having Hutch and an amazing support bubble around me that one way or another it would work out.

I had to feel the fear and do it anyway!

So, on the 13th June 2019, I delivered my last client presentation, packed up my desk, handed my security badge in and felt light as a feather as I walked (ok, very nearly skipped) out of that office.

Was it all unicorns and rainbows after?

I'd have been deluded to think that leaving the corporate world was going to miraculously change my life. But what it did do was give me a sense of weight being lifted, of having the headspace to think, to be able to breathe without feeling like the walls were closing in.

I gifted myself a week "off" before I went head strong into my new life as well as gifting myself a mini Mulberry, having never really fit in with the 'Mulberry handbag ladies' at work when I started.

I spent a lot of time reflecting on my twelve-year career in crisis management and how I could bring those lessons of resilience, facing the unknown and turning that fear into confidence into my business and more importantly to my brand photography clients. I began to see patterns within my clients, the inability for them to step into being visible, too afraid to show their person-ality and therefore shying away from the camera.

Because the phrases I hear most when it comes to having a shoot are

- I don't like being in front of the camera
- I don't know what to wear / I have nothing that looks good on me
- What if people laugh and think "who does she think she is?"
- I'm not photogenic
- I don't look good on camera
- What do I do with my hands / arms / legs (insert random body part here!)

And when I dig into where this is coming from, it's fear – that fear of the unknown is raising its ugly head again and attacking their confidence.

So, much like with my crisis clients, we put a plan in place, spend time getting to know their personality, their brand values, planning locations, props, clothes etc. Which means then there is nothing left "unknown" so that fear reduces and that confidence has space to grow. It grows even more once they see how amazing they are on camera (because that's what a photographer should do, show you how amazing you truly are and how everyone else already sees that).

I was flying at the end of 2019; it was everything I had hoped this new life would be. But then in came 2020, the year that was set to rock the boat, to trigger some of those wobbles, as I've seen in so many of my business friends.

The irony of a pandemic happening after I've left the world of crisis management has not been lost on me. It's the sort of crisis you spend years planning and training for, so to not be there to be part of the response was at first difficult. Having said that, not enough to lure me back in: thank you for the kind offers, but no thank you!

The fear of the unknown has ravaged through 2020. For some it's allowed them to thrive, to push themselves, to pivot and to try new things. For others, their industries have been whipped out from underneath them. I think I've been somewhere in the middle – to be honest not wanting to pivot to a purely online business yet. My passion is being behind the camera, but my experience of riots, bomb threats, flooding and everything else, along with the resilience I've built up over the years has certainly helped. It's what helped me deliver remote shoots (a strange and surreal experience, directing both the client and someone in their bubble with a camera – hard for a control freak like me!). I delivered training and courses to those in the wedding industry, guiding them in taking their own photos of their craft and demonstrating that they were able to still create income even though weddings were on hold. And due to the tenacity and creativity with my clients, I've still been able to photograph 43 women over 85 shoots whenever we've been allowed out!

And that's what I want people to know: you have the power and strength inside you to feel the fear and do it anyway. Sometimes you need to just take that jump, to feel the adrenaline of the next big step in order to thrive.

But without the incredible people to cheer me on and inspire me every step of the way, those wobbles could have brought the whole thing crumbling around me.

After every crisis there is a debrief, and as we come out of this one, I'll take stock to see what the next steps are, to build on that resilience, to see where I can put things in place to continue to grow and improve. To thank my lucky stars for the people around me and to remind myself that there are huge things out there, not only for me but also the amazing people who step in front of my camera.

And it's important to remember, we're all made of strong stuff.

Dig deep. Sometimes it's hiding and needs some coaxing out.

Whatever you set your mind to, you can do it and you will flourish.

If I can, then you can too.

ABOUT THE AUTHOR

Amanda Hutchinson

Amanda Hutchinson is a branding photography expert helping ambitious entrepreneurs and creatives to create compelling images for their business, so they can become visible to more of their perfect clients, make more money and feel confident and empowered in the process.

In addition to brand photography, Amanda is one half of a husband and wife wedding photography business, working with couples to tell their story and capture those emotions and moments.

As a successful Professional Photographer, Amanda's work, through her clients, has been featured in Forbes, national newspapers and magazines and has had commissions throughout both the UK and Europe.

Amanda is passionate about not only creating powerful images but in helping entrepreneurs to fight the fear of being in front of the camera, to stop them hiding from their own successes and embrace their brand.

CONTACT:

EMAIL: hello@amandakarenphotography.co.uk
WEBSITE: https://www.akpbrandingstories.co.uk/

facebook.com/AKPBrandingStories

instagram.com/akpbrandingstories

pinterest.com/AmandaKarenPhotography

linkedin.com/in/amanda-hutchinson-brand-photographer

3

BETHAN DAVIES

If You Believe You Can You Will

As I sit here on my extra-large snuggle chair with my snuggly blanket, about to write my chapter in this book, I think about how grateful I am to be sat here warm and cosy instead of in the car during rush hour traffic and the pouring down rain on my way to a busy shift at the hospital.

Just a year ago that's what I would have been doing. Working my guts out so I could scrimp and save for a yearly holiday for my family.

Now I sit here looking around at my lavish and totally free lifestyle, in complete awe and realisation of how far I've come and how very different my life started out in the beginning. To have a career in the hospital and a yearly holiday was alien to most of my family who are in council houses and never left little old Wales.

Now I'm on a different planet from them.

You see, I was never born to be this highly successful multiple business owner with a vastly growing property portfolio and a life I can proudly describe as enjoyable, calm and flexible (apart from while my three year old girl is in the room, of course, not always so calm then).

If someone had told my eighteen year old self that I'd be making multiple six figures a year at the age of 32 and making a MASSIVE difference to people's lives too, I would have thought they were high on drugs.

For now, let me tell you briefly about my pride and joy business. I have many businesses but this one is my baby. My coaching business stems from my passion and family values. You see, my life has gone to pretty dark places in the past and the only reason I survived and am here today is because of my family – my parents, my amazing husband and my baby girl and baby bump in my belly.

My family are everything to me. I know everyone says that, but truly, my family have been at the root of all my success and the core reason I push and fight for the best lifestyle imaginable to us. This passion for creating the dream family lifestyle runs so deep inside me that I turned this passion into a highly profitable business, helping families across the globe to turn their dream life into their reality too, because I strongly believe we only get one shot at a life and we have the control to make it the best life possible.

We can't control the curve balls that are thrown at us throughout life, but we can control how we deal with them and how we bounce back from them after they floor us.

Let me take you on a journey from where it all began for me and how I turned my life around, not because I want to jabber on about myself, but because I want you to see that no matter how difficult your life is, or how much you feel this dream life just isn't for people like you, I want you to see what IS POSSIBLE. Oh, what is truly possible. For me and for you. You'll see….

WHERE IT ALL BEGAN

Thinking back to my earliest childhood years, it was fun!

I lived with my mam, three brothers, uncle, cousins and grandparents all in my Nanny Val's small council house. It was on a small council estate and everyone knew everyone on the estate. We didn't have any money but us kids would have hours of fun playing on the mountain behind, climbing the rocks, swimming in the pond, giving the farmer grief so he would chase us off his land with his gun. Thinking back now, we were little terrors.

We were a very close family and had a tight knit group of friends too and we had each others' backs. There were so many of us none of the other kids would dare mess with one of us. It was such a fun and exciting childhood. We didn't need money.

Then things started to change…

My dad worked away most of my younger childhood. He was working so hard to get us a house of our own. Then one day, I remember him coming home and whisking me, my mam and brothers away to show us our very own house. It was like a fairy tale. I had my own bedroom and I was allowed to decorate it how I liked too. It was amazing.

Until it wasn't.

My dad still worked away through the week so we would spend the week at my nan's and then go home on weekend when my dad was home. He used to take us to different places every weekend. We went to different parks, zoos, caravan holidays. It was great, except as I grew older, I could see my cousins and friends looked at me differently. I wasn't the same as them. Their parents wouldn't even take them to the local park. My uncle drank a lot. That's what all the adults did on the estate. My dad was different: he set curfews for us and would ground us if we were home even five minutes late. None of my cousins or friends had curfews or got grounded. I grew to really resent my dad and his strict ways. Now I know he just wanted a better life for us.

DRUG ABUSE, OVERDOSE & SUICIDE

I was an exceedingly difficult teenager. I went off the rails, I was crazy, wild and uncontrollable. My cousins and friends loved to be around me. I was the most daring, I wasn't scared of anything, I was fun, and they loved me for it. Now, looking back I know I was just desperately trying to fit in and show them I wasn't different.

We drank all the time and took drugs and skipped school. I can't even bring myself to write some of the things we got up to. I'm not proud of my past but I can't regret it either. It all helped to shape me into the person I am today.

Things took a turn in my life when I was seventeen. I ran into some trouble and that's when I first realised I needed to calm down. Not long after this, things got dark. My cousin died of a drug overdose, my best friend hanged himself when he was high on drugs, my uncle died of liver failure and the list went on.

This was the first turning point in my life.

The devastation and pain my family were suffering hurt. I knew it could have just as easily been me. I couldn't put my parents through that pain and my Nanny Val had suffered enough. I wasn't going to be next and I wasn't to be the one to make her suffer even more, so I changed my life around. I stopped the drugs, I got myself a job in the hospital as an assistant in the X-ray department.

But I still didn't fit in there either.

They looked at me differently. I'm sure they could sense I grew up on a council estate. I recall one of the girls saying I was a bit rough. When I asked what she meant, she said she wouldn't mess with me. They made me feel like I wasn't as good as them. These girls were prim and proper, they had never taken drugs (I know, because they asked me if I ever had) and they hung out in nice places and bought nice things.

Most of my life up to this point I felt like I never really fitted in anywhere. I wondered why I couldn't fit in. I felt like there was something wrong with me, like I wasn't good enough.

I think this low self-esteem is what landed me in a bad relationship.

THE VIOLENCE AND TRUE TURNING POINT

He was a childhood boyfriend I had rekindled with. By this point I had lost my cousin, uncle, grandad and a few friends. Dick (not his real name) knew my cousin and grandad as he had stayed at my Nanny Val's house with us when we were teenagers. He knew how close I was with my cousin and hung out with us a few times. I think this gave me comfort that he knew the people I had lost who were very dear to me.

I think it was also that comfort that he knew the old me. I was far more sensible at this point and working a good job. He had escaped the valley and its troubles too. He was in the army. We got a house together and would go away as often as we could.

He hadn't really escaped his troubles though. He drank a lot and binged on drugs on the weekends. I turned a blind eye and pretended like I didn't know he did it. I had girls approaching me all the time saying he had been with them over the weekend. He always denied it, and I'm not sure to this day if I believed him or if I just ignored it. He always tried to pick arguments with me, right from the beginning, but I never gave into them. It was like I knew deep down not to bite back.

The first time I did answer back, he got violent.

I went and stayed at his parents because I couldn't face telling my parents or letting them see me. I haven't spoken to them to this day about how violent he was.

I stayed with him for quite some time after this. The violence got worse.

One night he had one of his violent outbursts and then stormed out. He usually went on a bender of booze and drugs and wouldn't return until the next morning. I sat there on the floor crying and crying until I couldn't cry anymore. I didn't know what to do. I couldn't take anymore.

The thought of ending my life crossed my mind. But I quickly dismissed that. There was no way I could put my parents and family through that pain. I'd seen that pain before. That was not an option.

This was a massive turning point in my life. I pretty much hit rock bottom before I could find the courage to take control and change things. I left him.

I moved back to my parents' house and then quickly moved country to run away from my life and start afresh. Amongst this chaos of a life I had been studying night school to get the qualifications to go to university and become a qualified Radiographer (I had to show I could be just as good as those stuck up girls I worked with).

I was trying to get into Cardiff University but had been rejected three years in a row. I applied last minute through clearing to a university in England and got in.

It was perfect timing. There was my escape.

I left everything behind: my money, my furniture, my clothes, everything. All I took from that life was a small bag of clothes, my phone and my laptop.

I started all over again.

LIGHT AT THE END OF THE TUNNEL

I worked three jobs around university to help pay for my accommodation and living expenses. I worked nights and studied all day. It was tough, but I loved it. I had never felt so free in all of my life. During holidays and most weekends my house mates would rush off home and that was my favourite time, the peace and quiet and the house all to myself.

I loved being alone.

Three years went by and this whole experience changed me completely. I felt so strong and independent. I had ideas of travelling the world working in x-ray departments in different countries, experiencing different cultures. I had no interest in moving back to my old town, ever. I was seeing my parents and brothers regularly, a few of my good friends from home visited me in England and we stayed in touch. But I had no intention of moving back to the Rhondda Valleys.

Until I met Lee of course (my now husband). We met just before I graduated. It was at a pub in the Rhondda when I had come home to attend a ladies' charity night with friends. Don't ask me why he and his mates were at a ladies' night.

The one and only reason I agreed to a night out in the Rhondda was because it was a ladies' night and for charity. I wouldn't have dared have a night out in the Rhondda otherwise. I think deep down I feared running into the ex (Dick as we call him for this chapter). Plus I didn't want to mingle with valleys boys. They were no good in my eyes.

Anyway, obviously Lee won me over. It certainly wasn't love at first sight. It took quite some time for me to agree to go on a date with him. He tried for quite some time, bless him. I'm so glad he was so persistent. At the time I could never have imagined having such a happy life with a valleys boy.

Lee and his friends were so different from the other valleys boys I knew, though. Totally different. They were just as fun and wild, but they were respectful. They were a decent group of boys with really good morals. A bit like my dad, really.

As soon as I gave in and started dating Lee, it didn't take long before I was completely hooked and knew he was my future. His friends became my friends and we travelled to different countries together. My parents even joined us and got on great with the boys too.

They came to Cuba with us where Lee and I got married.

I know this sounds weird, but Lee's friends played a huge part in sealing the deal for me and Lee. They made me feel like I fitted in. For the first time in my life I actually felt like I belonged.

Life was so good. An amazing husband, supportive family and good friends, a career I was so proud of, a mortgage, a nice car and a beautiful baby girl.

I even set a savings up for my parents' retirement, to help them retire comfortably and repay them for all the help and support they'd given me all my life.

Life was perfect.

Until it wasn't.

THE (NOT SO) PERFECT QUALIFIED JOB

When Aria was almost a year old, I was coming to the end of my maternity leave. That's when I started looking into options to work from home. I didn't want to quit my job, I loved my job, I just wanted to reduce the hours so I could spend more time at home with my baby girl. But I needed to replace that financial loss from dropping my hours.

In fact, I wanted to make more money to help with child-care costs and all the amazing things I wanted to do with my little family. I wanted regular holidays, I wanted to be able to spend comfortably on new clothes, I wanted to be able to eat out more. I couldn't though, not with the house and car bills and the costs that come with a growing child.

Then Coaching By Beth was born, my baby business, my pride and joy.

As my coaching business grew, I started to see many faults and flaws in my perfect qualified job. It suddenly wasn't so perfect. I struggled to get the days off that I wanted because others were wanting the same days holidays. There was barely any flexibility around childcare and it was torture having to work on my baby girl's first Christmas. It broke my heart.

I swore I would never work another Christmas.

I tried to reduce my hours more but they wouldn't let me. I was contracted thirty hours but was working more because we were so short staffed.

It was also quite difficult dealing with all the negativity I received from family and friends when I started looking for ways to work from home. They couldn't understand why I was willing to give up my amazing career to be a stay at home mum. Thing is, I'd happily be a stay at home mum if I had the finances to live the life I want to live. So I kept working on my coaching business and hoped that I would be able to reduce my hospital hours soon. Thing is, though, it was tricky to put the time into growing the business when I was working around the clock.

Then I got pregnant.

It was perfect timing really, because the maternity leave would give me the time I needed to grow my business and I would be in a better position to negotiate fewer hours when returning to work. I still didn't want to quit my job, I really enjoyed it. I just wanted two days a week, that would have been ideal.

Then life threw a curve ball.

THE MISCARRIAGE AND FINAL STRAW

We lost our baby when I was thirteen weeks pregnant.

Nothing could have prepared me for the roller coaster that was to follow.

I had known so many women to have miscarriages and never really thought of it as a big deal, until it happened to me. I never understood the depth of that invisible pain a woman suffers when she loses a baby. It hit me so hard.

I had experienced so much pain in the past but it was a totally different kind of pain. Worse really. I felt so lonely too, because there weren't many people who I felt understood my pain. People started to make me feel so damn annoyed by their comments.

"It's ok for you because you already have a daughter."

"You're young, plenty of time for another."

"Better now at thirteen weeks: some women have a stillborn."

"It wasn't really a baby though, more a foetus at that stage."

I wanted to scream and shout at people's ignorance and complete idiocy. I wanted to tell them to shut the hell up and keep their stupid opinions to themselves. I had never felt such anger and annoyance.

But after reflecting, I realise, I've probably made at least one of those comments in the past myself. People don't usually say things with intent to hurt us in these situations. I think when we are experiencing this kind of pain in life, any words can hurt, regardless of them being intended to make you feel better.

The worst part was going back to work. I'd heard that some colleagues had passed comment about me being seen online with my coaching business when I was supposed to be off work sick. It really hurt to hear that. My coaching business really helped pull me through such a difficult time. It was the only thing I felt I could do. I couldn't face family, I couldn't face friends, I couldn't face work. I hid away for weeks and the only people I spoke to were online through my coaching business. It brought me comfort. It was the only thing that brought me comfort.

I felt like my boss and some work colleagues changed towards me. They felt cold, unsympathetic and made me feel so rubbish about myself. They made me feel like I was being silly and needed to get over it. My boss got really difficult with me over childcare and wanted me to work impossible hours and would not accommodate me at all, like he had done in the past.

I was worth more than that. I quit my job.

It was the best decision I could have made. Not that it felt like I had a choice, mind. It forced me to throw myself 100% into my coaching business and that's when my life really changed for the better.

My coaching business boomed, we invested in another business (the pub that Lee and I first met in), we bought a food/catering business, and we extended our property portfolio and have a small letting business too. Now most people think all these businesses must make me super duper busy. I hear it all the time! But that couldn't be further from the truth.

I have more flexibility and freedom now than I could have possibly dreamed of.

We have a caravan over in West Wales and spend much of our time over there. I only work during school hours and take days off to shop or eat out with friends as often as I like. I barely work during school holidays at all.

I've managed to accomplish this because I've set up smart income streams, businesses that can run themselves without needing much attention from me. My main focus is my little family and my coaching clients. But working with my clients doesn't even feel like work. It feels like I'm helping out friends, guiding them to a lifestyle of flexibility and freedom. I love my work and it completely fits around my family life, which was what I dreamt of.

I actually went shopping the other day to get some Christmas presents and came home with absolutely nothing for anyone else. I'd spend £400 all on myself. You know what, for the first time in my life, I didn't even feel guilty for spending on myself. I felt amazing. Usually the guilt would set in if I even so much as spent £50 on myself because that would be £50 I could have spent on my baby girl or put towards savings for a holiday. I've always dreamt of a life where I feel so comfortable that I can spend on what I want when I want and not feel bad about it because it wouldn't mean sacrificing other things, and I'm finally in that position.

I used to think that this kind of life was just fairy tales. I didn't truly believe it could exist for me. My life started out in such a different place. We had nothing. I look at some of my cousins and old friends and they still live that life I lived as a kid. The council estate, the drink and drugs. I don't think their kids have ever had a holiday or left little old Wales. They seem happy enough. Are they truly happy? I don't know. But I was never destined to live a life that couldn't make me truly happy.

I was taught from a very young age it's ok to be different, to have respect, and to work for the life I really wanted. Although I resisted it so much when I was growing up, I can never express how grateful I am to my parents for fighting for a better life for me.

There's a part of me that will always be that cheeky potty mouth council estate girl. Lee loves that part of me that very few people get to see. Mostly people see this highly driven, successful business woman. They've no idea of who I really am and where I have come from. It's not an act, and I'm not pretending to be someone I'm not (which I have been accused of, by the way), this is me. I like to be respectful and well-mannered around people, it's not an act, it's a choice.

I've lived almost my whole life feeling like the outsider, like I don't fit in, so now I really cherish my close relationships. I can count on my one hand my close girlfriends. They've been there since I was that wild teen. These girls, and my close family know me, and they don't care if they're talking to prim and proper Beth or potty mouth Beth, because they know that's just me and they love and accept me either way.

It took some work to be able to truly accept who I am and love myself, but this is what really helped me to change my life around. This is the key to my success really. My favourite saying is….

If you believe you can – You Will.

The first and most important step to creating your perfect life is to learn to love yourself for who you really are. Only then can you accept the love of others and feel worthy to live that perfect life.

I hold no shame about my past or where I come from.

I stopped caring what others think about me or who others expect me to be.

I put myself first.

I took care (and still take care) of me first.

Because how else can I be the very best I can be for my family if I don't take care of me?

There are two things I would love for anyone reading this to have really opened their mind to. The first is to realise that anything is possible for you and your future. The second is to realise that it's time to accept yourself and love yourself for who you are, for all the faults and the shame or guilt that you've ever felt. It's time to accept those things and love that they have made you the person you are today. The beautiful person you are.

When we accept our past, we can look to our future and make it the best imaginable.

I'm proof of that, and so are all the amazing women I've collaborated with for this book.

If we can pivot and create such success for ourselves, then so can you.

ABOUT THE AUTHOR

Bethan Davies

Bethan Davies is a multiple business owner and business coach whose sole mission is to help family passionate women create the lifestyle of flexibility and freedom that they desire, just like she has done for herself.

Beth generates a multiple six figure annual income from smart income streams such as properties, offline businesses and business coaching. Beth's zone of genius is creating income in smart ways which allows her to work fewer hours while earning more income. She currently works fewer than twenty hours a week.

Her values are heavily founded around family and her mission in life is to show ambitious business mums across the globe that there are smarter ways of creating income from their business whilst working fewer hours, so they can spend more of their time doing the things they love with their family.

Beth's Business Academy has gone global supporting mumpreneurs across the UK, USA and Canada. Her passion and mission for mumpreneurs across the globe has been supported by and featured in many credible sources such as the BBC, Dare Superdrug, Woman's Own, Women in Business Radio and many more.

CONTACT:

EMAIL: info@coachingbybeth.co.uk
WEBSITE: www.coachingbybeth.co.uk
FACEBOOK GROUP: www.facebook.com/
groups/mumpreneurfreedomhub/

facebook.com/coachingbybethan
instagram.com/coachingbybethan

CHELLE SHOHET

Mirror Mirror

Mirror mirror on the wall, who is the fairest of them all?

These were the words that would haunt me for years!

Thankfully, these days I look at myself in the mirror and I smile, I celebrate. I actually say thank you. Because I now love every inch, every curve, every lump and bump and every wobble of my body!

I'm sure if you asked most girls growing up around the same time as me, or even many little girls growing up today, most would see themselves as the princess, Snow White. But not me. What I saw reflected was myself as the evil queen. Think, if you would, of the scene in the Disney animation film when the queen's reflection is that of the ugly older woman. As I grew up, when I looked in the mirror what was reflected to me was ugly.

What was reflected to me was deep hate and disgust.

Throughout my teens, I grew up not wanting to see my reflection and avoiding full-length mirrors wherever possible. I would hide under towels in changing rooms, lock myself in bathrooms to change when at friends' houses, feeling very, very deep hate towards myself and my body.

Outwardly I appeared very confident and comfortable in my own body. I wore miniskirts and belly tops to keep up with the trends of that time. I loved heels and makeup. I went to dance classes and did dance shows and presentations in flamboyant dresses and leotards. I appeared to be just like any of the other girls around me.

But the truth was as far away from this as it was possible to be. Inside I felt so ugly. And it wasn't only the way I looked. I hated the way I thought, as well as the way I felt. It was impossible to escape.

A few years ago, I was caught by surprise when I had a rare day to myself and took myself off for a day of shopping. Now, as a stylist and personal shopper as well as a busy mum and wife, not to mention our other businesses, this is not something I manage to do that often. Not like this at any rate.

I had a whole day when I could go and have a leisurely wander around the shopping mall. I had a lovely champagne lunch and got to try on some clothes in peace and quiet at my favourite shops and boutiques. I hadn't done this in so long! It was bliss.

This surprise happened when I was in a changing room trying on some gorgeous underwear sets when I looked in this huge, full-length, ornate mirror.

This was the first time in years I was alone with myself. Not stressed, not rushed or preoccupied—just me with myself. As I looked at myself in the mirror, I could feel the deep, luxurious, plush carpet beneath my bare feet. I took a moment to look at this very opulent changing room I found myself in, with its long velvet drapes and couch, and Hollywood style lights surrounding the mirror.

For the first time in I do not know how long I stopped, and I looked at me.

I looked at my feet, my ankles, my muscular calves and my knees. As my eyes reached above my knees, I found myself turning my body to see my side reflection and running my hands to stroke and caress the soft skin of my thighs and then my curvy bottom before my tummy and hips. And as my eyes moved up my body, so did my hands. I was exploring and physically connecting with my body. I cupped my breasts and hugged my arms. I stroked my shoulders and then my neck and ran my fingers through my hair.

I noticed every lump and bump, I examined every scar and stretch mark and I smiled. This glorious, curvaceous, sexy, womanly body before me was and is my body. I smiled because every lump and bump, every scar and stretch mark told a story, my body story. And I am who I am today because of my body story.

That day as I looked at myself in that ornate changing room, I felt like a queen. I felt so proud of myself, of my body and what I and my body had achieved. I realised at that moment how far I had come.

I could feel the cold air coming from the gap under the door hitting my skin and the goosebumps that appeared; I could taste the champagne I was drinking and feel the fizzy bubbles on my tongue. I could feel the chilled glass flute I was holding in my hand. I was obsessed with how amazing it felt to run my long fingernails over my skin and how the silk and lace underwear I was trying on felt against my bare skin. And as I looked myself in the eye I felt alive, deeply connected to myself and my body, I loved what I was seeing and I felt energized and invigorated. If I am honest, it was pretty intoxicating!

Boy, was this a world away from how I felt in and about my body in my teens and my early twenties.

I went through many years of my life, burying my thoughts and feelings. I became an expert in doing so. I was a queen of ignoring pain, ignoring emotions and being strong so that I could survive whatever lay around the corner.

I remember when in my twenties, I was in yet another toxic relationship. I woke up one day and realised I was isolated from my friends and family, I had believed a whole cock and bull story my then-boyfriend had fed me, and I was in the USA, and there I was with no friends, no family and no fairytale story either. And I needed to figure something out and fast.

I remembered that when I packed my case, I had packed something, something that when I arrived in the USA and unpacked I wasn't quite sure why I had brought them with me. My Dancer Shoes. These very high, clear Perspex shoes were my answer. You see, a couple of years before this point I had done a stint of dancing in strip clubs as well as some modelling and some ring girl jobs in the UK.

I had held on to my shoes, and when I packed up all my stuff ready to head off to this dream adventure in the States, instead of getting rid of them or putting them in storage with my many boxes, I packed them in my bag to take with me. Why, I really didn't know, but I suppose something inside of me, you might call it my intuition, something said that they had to come too!

As I sat crying in my dirty motel room, realising I was in a do or die situation with my back up against the wall, metaphorically speaking, these dancer shoes felt like my saving grace.

That lunchtime I went out and used my last bit of cash and got some skimpy underwear and found out where the best gentlemen's clubs in town were.

I rolled up at the first club and auditioned, got the job and started an hour later. That night I worked 12+ hours and came home with a couple of thousand dollars in my pocket. I was exhausted, both physically and mentally.

The next few weeks were fun. I worked all the hours I could. I made new friends and started to feel stronger in myself. I hadn't realised just how down and depressed I had got or how isolated I had become. I wanted to find a way to part ways with my then-boyfriend, but that was proving difficult.

Another thing that I found really tough was how I felt about myself and my body. I had always struggled with my body image from a long list of harmful and toxic experiences I had had as a teen. But now I was dressing in these sexy underwear sets and dresses, with full-on hair and makeup, fake tan and all the things! I was doing this almost every night of the week so that I could take to that stage and strip it all off for the delight of the audience. What I found I couldn't do was look at myself and see my own beauty beneath all the makeup, self-tan and costumes.

I quickly got to the point where I couldn't leave my apartment without my makeup on and hair done anymore. I was obsessed with what I ate and about my weight and working out. In reality, with the amount I was dancing, I didn't need to worry, but I just couldn't see that. All I could see was this ugly, ugly reflection looking back at me.

But It wasn't just the way I looked, it was the way I thought and the way I felt. I hated my voice plus I hated my clothes and my hair… the list was never-ending. My relationship with my then-boyfriend was already toxic, but now it became even worse. And added to that, I was also turning on myself too. When I looked in the mirror, I would pick out all the negative things I could see. And I would really beat myself up about them. The things I would say to myself and about myself were so derogatory and damaging.

At this time, I was convinced that I was getting fat and that I needed a boob job and lipo along with a nose job and my eyes changed. I even had several appointments with plastic surgeons. More than one suggested I should speak to a therapist about how I felt about my body before I made any changes or underwent any surgery.

Thank god, they didn't just let me book in right there and then! But I didn't get round to doing the therapy because I was too busy and had better things to do.

Or I wasn't ready to do the surgery yet, so when I was, then I would sort out the therapy. All excuses, of course!

Looking back on it now, I was petrified. I was petrified not of the surgery but of the therapist and them telling me that I was crazy. And of the surgeon confirming that I actually needed even more work done than I thought I needed.

Believe it or not, I thought I was really positive, and I feared that the truth was that I was a lot worse than I had convinced myself. I didn't trust what I saw in the mirror. I believed the negative things I felt and thought about myself so much that I feared I was kidding myself and was even worse than I could imagine.

But each day I went to work, I danced my butt off, and I earned really good money. So I found myself caught in this strange place. Because as time went on, I started working in more clubs all over the States. I was managing to work in some of the very sought after clubs, clubs that had very high standards. They were very strict when it came to how their dancers looked, to the point that when I once had a cold and took a few days off, and I turned up to work the following week without having gone for a fake tan top-up, the management pulled me aside and told me to go and get my tan done the next morning, or I couldn't work the following night.

So I logically knew that I must be somewhat attractive. Looking around me, I was surrounded every day by stunning women, and I was earning as well if not better than many of them.

But when I looked in the mirror, especially when I wasn't working, when I didn't have makeup on, I really struggled to see anything nice let alone anything beautiful.

I soon started to dissociate the me when I was working and dancing and the me when I wasn't.

When I was dancing, I was my alter ego, Morgan. That was my stage name. I was confident, chatty, funny and could give as good as I got.

When I was just me, Chelle, out of work, I was quiet, more reserved, anxious, shy and nervous. But as time passed, my view of myself got even more toxic. And the way I felt about myself became even more harmful, and so my alter ego Morgan became a permanent feature whenever I was out and about. It was a way that I could avoid looking at myself and acknowledging how I was feeling, a way to protect myself.

To the outside world, I was living the high life. I was making good money. I was going on amazing trips. I was travelling to new places and experiencing new adventures. I was also working on other projects. And for well over a year, just short of two, I managed to hold it together and build what seemed like quite a sweet life. But the honest truth was I was dying inside.

Then one day, I had to do a photoshoot. I needed pictures of me for work, and I also wanted to get images of the dresses I had designed and had made for dancing. Most of

the women I worked with would buy dresses and underwear sets that were sold in dancers' shops and in the
changing rooms of clubs up and down the country. It was
a big business. Every dancer was competing with every
other dancer every night. So having new outfits and
keeping your look fresh and polished was essential to your
success as a dancer. And as a designer I loved designing
and creating unique dresses that stood out. They were
loud and different from all the rest and helped me
stand out.

When I took to the stage, I would do pole dancing and do
pole tricks, and I would put on a show. And very quickly
this included my outfits, dresses and underwear sets. It was
all part of the show. This always went down well with the
club management and audience too. And I built a bit of a
fan base at a few of the clubs.

So I needed to get some photos done as I was receiving
invites to visit different clubs. I also wanted to start to
show off my dress designs as I was using them in my stage
shows and some other girls were beginning to show
interest in them. And I started to think maybe I could start
a business and sell my dresses too. I began to dream of a
life beyond dancing. I had massive dreams!

The day of the photoshoot came, and I was so excited. I
had new dresses made, and had my hair and makeup
done. I was feeling good. As the shoot was going on I was
having fun, and I was confident that the images would

look stunning. And then I looked at the pictures. And I hated them. I was heartbroken.

Everyone around me was waxing lyrical about how amazing I looked and how good the pictures looked. But I couldn't see what everyone around me was saying. And my then-boyfriend saw this and used it also to put the boot in. He didn't like me finding this newfound confidence and having my own money or having ambitions that didn't include him. So when I looked at them, I saw myself as fat, I saw myself as ugly and odd-looking. I was convinced I looked like a kid rather than a woman. I couldn't see sexy; I saw frumpy. I couldn't see sultry; I saw awkward and boyish. All these things were backed up and reiterated by this boyfriend because it served his own agenda.

Looking at these images also stirred up a whole load of negative feelings that, looking back on them now I can see, I had really worked hard to bury and had avoided feeling for many, many years. Feelings of hate, disgust, shame and fear, all the dark and heavy feelings and emotions you can think of, were stirred up deep inside, and I really struggled to manage my thoughts and feelings.

I was drinking more and becoming more obsessive about my body and about work, and I was taking more risks at work too. Working in clubs that I had avoided because they had made me feel uneasy or uncomfortable in the past, taking more risks when doing pole tricks and drinking more too. I was working longer and harder and pushing myself both physically and emotionally to the brink. I was becoming consumed by this hate I had for myself and my body.

And one night it all came to ahead. By this time, I felt I had been in a very, very dark place for some weeks. And instead of going to work that night, I went for a walk across the bridge near the club. I was in a really dark place where I found myself disassociated from myself and my body. It was like I was watching it happen to me, but I had no control whatsoever.

I don't quite know what I was thinking or planning as it is still to this day a bit of a blur. But I know that in that day before getting ready for work I had got in the shower and washed my hair a dozen times because I kept forgetting I had washed it and I wanted to wash out all these heavy, suffocating feelings I had. I rubbed my skin raw with my exfoliate, and my face stung after I lost count of the times I had washed my face. But I could barely feel it at the time.

The reason I know that my skin was rubbed raw and my face was sore and irritated is because when I was sitting on the edge of that bridge that night a very kind person stopped and offered me a helping hand. I can still to this day remember their scent. It was really strong, and it was as though this helped snap me out of this dark trance-like state I was in. They sat with me and talked to me and helped me come around from this terrifying disassociated state I had been in. They helped me cry, they helped me laugh, and they helped me feel those feeling just a little for just a moment. And at that moment I realised it was possible to feel again. It was possible to be alive again. And I didn't want to die.

That night a dancer friend also came to my aid. They let me stay with them, and they shared their night's earnings with me so that I didn't have to tell my then-boyfriend what had happened. They helped me take care of the sores I had on my legs and my arms from where I had scrubbed so hard that afternoon. They helped me see to my redraw face caused by washing my face so much. And they helped me reconnect with me, my feelings, my emotions and my body again in the weeks and months that followed. They became my very best friend. They listened and they held me when I cried my eyes out. They helped me believe and they helped me take away the pain by being kind and loving to my body.

Back in that luxurious changing room as I sipped champagne and admired my body in the mirror, I remembered those pictures, and I remembered how much I loathed my body at that time. I thought about how dark my thoughts and feelings had gone—both about myself and the way I viewed and felt about my body. I remembered feeling so disconnected, feeling such hatred; it felt so heavy and so all-encompassing! And I remembered looking out at sea

from that bridge that night and how I didn't feel any love
for myself or my body.

But here I am some eleven years later. I am fit and healthy,
looking at my body in a full length mirror. The same body
as I had back then, but not only do I love my body, I
accept my body, lumps, bumps, scars and stretch marks
and all. It is a fact and there is no denying it, I am much
curvier now than I was then. Back then I was a UK Size
2. On that day in front of that ornate mirror, I was a UK
Size 10. But the truth was and is that I love my body more
today than I ever did as that very slender dancer. I have
more respect and compassion today for myself, my
thoughts, my feelings and my emotions. I also have more
respect and gratitude for my body and all the experiences
I have had.

It hasn't been a straightforward journey to being confident
and having self-love and acceptance. Far from it! There
have been emergency surgeries that saved my life but saw
me balloon to a size 12-14 overnight and dropped me into
a deep depression. There have been pregnancies and an
emergency c section, as well as a couple of cancer scares,
and hormonal issues that have all affected my body, its
shape and its size.

But I have also cycled 450KM across China in five days,
eighteen months after emergency surgery, as well as
successfully running two half marathons in recent years. I
have carried a baby to term and managed to breastfeed

him. I have lost weight and gained weight. My body has countless stories that once upon a time I was so ashamed of. So embarrassed that I hated my body with such conviction and venom.

But in that moment on the bridge when I woke up from my dissociative state and realised I wanted to live, and in the moment I woke up in intensive care after surgery, I promised myself I would forever be grateful for my life and my body. As well as this day standing in this changing room admiring my body and realising that I really do love my body! And I really do love myself inside and out.

But what was even bigger than that? As I stood looking in this full-length mirror, I realised I want to have an impact. I want to help other women who have stood in front of a mirror or looked at a picture and felt that despair, self-loathing and hatred of themselves, felt shame or disgust about themselves and their bodies just like I have. It might have been all-consuming or even just a little bit.

I want to help women who have important stories to share or amazing gifts to get out into the world. Women who want to leave a legacy and an impact in the world like I do. I want to help those women to look and feel like their best selves and be confident in their own skin, have confidence in their own thoughts, feelings and emotions, so that they can show up, so that they can trust themselves, their thoughts, feelings and emotions. So that they can have unshakable confidence in themselves and how they show up.

And if I want to change the way our children truly, and in turn their children, view themselves and their bodies then I have to own my story. I have to be willing to share the good, the bad and the ugly of my journey to having confidence as well as self-love and acceptance, so that I can inspire, support other women to do the same.

And so it was, as I sipped champagne and tried on a gorgeous bodysuit and stockings that made me feel sexy and hugged me and all my curves in all the right places, I made a promise to myself that I would find a way to share. I would open up and help others feel the same joy I feel now as I look at my body, and feel the confidence I have in myself now.

I decided at that moment, some years ago now, that if I wanted to really help and have the sort of impact I dream of, then I needed to refine my process and I needed to distill what I have done for myself but also what I have helped countless other women achieve too.

As I started to work on this and to build clarity around the impact I wanted to have in the world and the legacy I wanted to leave, I realised that my journey had been one triggered by choices.

As I learned how to reconnect with my own body, I learned that it all starts with me reconnecting with my mind, my thoughts and my feelings first. I had to choose to reconnect. If I was thinking and talking to myself negatively, aggressively, derogatively, and indignantly, then when I looked at myself I had already set the tone for how I would view myself. And this in turn also dictated how I treat myself too. But I could choose to change this.

I also realised that when you're working on the inside it's so valuable to simultaneously work on the outside too. You can use your wardrobe as a tool, not only to reconnect but to discover and to grow in confidence. I used my wardrobe, my style and my image as a daily practice to reconnect with myself and to check in on how I was feeling. It also became a tool and a reminder to me when things slipped too. I made a choice to use the clothes I was wearing as a form of self-care.

So If I am really negative etc. and I then look at myself in a mirror, I will unconsciously as well as consciously see all the negatives. I will also be more likely to assume the worst and believe the negative at first instance. I am also more likely to hide behind my clothes and use them to prove the negative and derogatory conversation I am having with myself inside my head. Or I could choose to wear clothes that I love and challenge my thoughts and feelings when I don't catch them in time.

This mindset and these thought processes will then have an effect on the way you will see, view and treat yourself in all areas of life as well as your body. It can have far-reaching effects just like the ripple effects of a stone being dropped in a puddle of water.

The experiences and traumas I experienced as a child and as a teen set the tone for how I felt about myself, how I reacted to myself, my thoughts and my emotions for the first two decades of my life and into the third decade too. And they, in turn, affected how I viewed myself and my body as well how I treated myself and my body.

And it has taken a lot of work and dedication to rewire my thoughts, beliefs, habits and practices about me and my body. It has not always been easy nor has it been fun at times, I grant you, but it has been worth it!

Because the way you view yourself and the way you treat yourself dictates how you will eventually view and treat your loved ones around you. How you interact with yourself will affect how you interact with others and how you allow others to treat you too. That's even more of a reason to take a moment and realise that for me, for you, for us, to achieve our goals, our dreams and our ambitions, then we need to invest some time and effort into how we view and treat ourselves and our bodies. To safeguard and ultimately skyrocket our future successes.

If I can change the way I view myself and my body and now feel confident in my own skin, confident in my own thoughts and feelings as well as in my emotions, the good and not so good, then I know you can too!

Is it time for you to shine? Are you ready to look and feel amazing? Are you ready to be confident in your own skin, confident in your own thoughts and your own feelings? Then it's time you take a look in that mirror and do what I did and what my clients do. Make a commitment to yourself to make a change. And come and join me as we help women and girls change the way they view and treat themselves and their bodies forever!

ABOUT THE AUTHOR

Chelle Shohet

Chelle Shohet is an International Stylist and Coach, a certified One of Many Women's Coach, a Speaker, Fashion Designer, Multiple Business Owner, Co-Author of Amazon No1 Bestseller, She Who Dares, Mother, Wife, Sister and Friend with a passion for helping people.

She specialises in working with speakers, entrepreneurs and women who want to look and feel more stylish, more confident and ultimately become more visible in life and business.

She supports real women with real bodies to truly love and embrace their minds, bodies and souls, helping them to connect and fall in love with themselves inside and out.

By combining the inner and outer work, Chelle takes the sting out of personal styling and unlocks a woman's inner confidence, making it tangible and achievable for every woman!

Working with Chelle, women develop a deep understanding of their physical, mental and emotional needs as well as discovering and developing their true style, bringing to life a true reflection of them, their personality, and passions without them needing to say a word.

This is a truly holistic experience - not just a style makeover but a whole life makeover.

Supporting women to embrace looking and feeling amazing inside and out has become Chelle's mission due to her own personal transformation. Chelle knows first-hand about the effects of low self-esteem, lack of confidence and poor body image. She has also experienced and recovered from burnout during her time in corporate, giving her a unique understanding of how today's world and its unique challenges affect women, their minds, their bodies and their soul.

By working on the inside as well as the outside, Chelle helps her clients to achieve the instant gratification we all desire while also laying the solid foundations that will empower them to build and evolve from robust and unshakable confidence and believe in themselves, helping them develop and master the art of managing their own energy, balance and emotions. Chelle has found this invaluable in her own life.

Chelle is on a quest to share her skills and learnings with at least one million women by 2025. She hopes they will in turn share them onwards with each and every woman and girl they know.

Her mission in life is to change the way every woman and girl views and treat themselves so that they can grow and flourish in this world of filters and social media by being entirely confident in their own skin!

CONTACT:

EMAIL: Chelle@ChelleShohet.com
WEBSITE: https://www.chelleshohet.com/

facebook.com/chelle.shohet
instagram.com/chelleshohet
linkedin.com/in/chelleshohet

5

DIANE IVORY

QUIT BEFORE IT'S SHIT

"Again, again! Pleeeease!"

"No. Another time. It's time to stop now. Back into your Sixes."

I lost count of how many times I uttered those words at the Scout Hut in the grounds of The Church of the Good Shepherd where I was a Cub Scout leader for the 12th Carshalton Cub Scouts, more years ago than I care to remember.

I was "Akela". The one who stood in the middle of the room encircled by crouching boys aged 7-11, all promising to do their best. That, after all, is all we should expect of ourselves and of each other; I was proud of the many young men who were temporarily in my care over the course of fifteen or so years.

How I came to be a Cub Scout leader in charge of a "pack" of boys when I was just eighteen is a story for another time, but many of the lessons I learned from that time in my life have stayed with me ever since.

Notably, the one where I realised that if we played a game that they loved for too long they would tire of it and the magic of playing it another day would be lost. So, I always stopped before they had had enough. While it was still fun. In so doing it was a treat when we played the same game in subsequent weeks.

I'm sure that all the games we played back then would be banned now on grounds of health and safety, but it was the 1980s. There was nothing wrong with playing games like British Bulldog, where the aim of the game is to get from one side of the room to the other without being floored by the opposing team. How the game was never stopped by the cries of a child with a broken limb I'll never know, but I do know it was always what they wanted to play. And I let them. For just long enough. Never for too long.

I took this lesson from the Scout hut and into life outside. I still carry it with me now. For instance, I like to leave a party before I see the room emptying. I like to go while I am still having a good time. A bit like Cinderella on a curfew and running away from the ball before she wanted to – only I am not on a curfew and it's my choice to go early. Incidentally, I have never left a shoe behind and am STILL waiting to find my Prince Charming!

Don't get me wrong, I LOVE a party and there were many times in my youth when I woke the next day to find myself sleeping on the floor under whatever I could find to cover me, but this became far less appealing and not the least bit fun nor adventurous as I got older.

I left education while I was still enjoying it too. I wasn't a great scholar, but I was a great socialiser and had lots of friends at the all-girls school I attended. I am sure that the absence of boys was a bonus for me – I'm easily distracted and would have paid even less attention to the lessons if there had been boys in the room! As it is, I have very fond memories of my school days and still meet up with a group of school friends for a reunion lunch each year. It is fun to catch up and get snippets of each others' lives. Boyfriends and husbands have come and gone. Children have brought us angst and joy in equal measure as we have nurtured them till they were ready to fly the nest. Jobs, joys and woes; parents getting old and feisty, sick and sadly passing on. We have been through it all alone yet together and an annual catch up takes us back to more carefree times.

I lost my Dad when I was 29. My parents had divorced when I was sixteen and my brother and I had lived with him after my Mum left. If I was poorly and not feeling well enough to go to school, I'd ask him what he thought. He always replied, "Only you know how you feel. You have to decide." I just wanted him to make the decision for me, to tell me I looked shocking and to give me permission to stay off. But he wouldn't. The decision always lay with me and probably meant that I went in when I really wasn't well enough to. Surely if I had looked THAT bad, he would have told me to stay at home. If he didn't, I assumed he thought I should go!

Looking back, the first even vaguely major decisions I made were my O and A Level choices. This wasn't too hard. I just chose what I was best at, and as I wasn't brilliant at any of it this wasn't too tricky!

Although I was always top of the class in my primary school it had just come naturally, and I had never really learnt how to study. Once I reached the third year at high school it soon became apparent that my "top of the class" days were over and that Uni life probably wasn't going to fit into my plans.

Did I say plans? Hmmmm. Well, I didn't really have any plans. Some might say I lacked ambition. I would say I was keeping my options open.

Truth is, I just wasn't driven. I didn't have anything I desperately wanted to do. I had toyed with becoming a radiographer and spent my two weeks' work experience in the diagnostic radiography department at the Royal Marsden Hospital.

I wasn't filled with joy doing during my time there, so when my A level predictions weren't great, I just accepted them and forgot any idea of a career in radiography. After leaving school with a handful of A Levels it was time to find a job.

It was 1983. Unemployment was at its highest level since the depression of the 1920s and jobs were hard to come by. I did a stint working in the men's shirts department at Marks and Spencer that Christmas. Fun times, but not something I wanted to do long term. Again, someone more driven might have seen the opportunities that could come working for such a well-known organisation. Work hard. Impress the management. Become the management.

This didn't even occur to me. Besides, I was there as a "temporary seasonal" and whilst a few would be taken on as full-time staff after the season was over, I had already decided that it wasn't for me. I had another decision to make.

I had been offered a job as a lab technician in a school. The lab techs in my school had been incredibly old and doddery. It was always touch and go as to who would be first to break a glass beaker; them or us. I was at the other end of the spectrum. Just eighteen and not much older than the oldest students there.

I enrolled on a part time course at Paddington Technical College and started studying for a BTEC in Science Laboratory Technology. I was given a day off each week to attend under the "day release" scheme. BTECs were new. They were introduced in 1984 and seen by many as the "poor man's" A level. Less so now, as time has allowed them to demonstrate how beneficial vocational courses are, with hands-on learning in some subjects being far more useful than the more academic A Levels.

I took the course, though I don't feel the decision to do so was mine. More something I had to do as part of the job. Another decision made for me, not by me. So there I was, working in a job I fell into rather than chose because it was the only thing I could get at the time. Embarking on a course that I'd not chosen but felt I had to do.

Little did I know that I would make my first TV appearance at this college. It was in 1986 and the BBC came along to show a clip of the "AIDS – Don't Die of Ignorance" campaign. I had said something relevant and punchy which they liked and asked me to say it again while they filmed it. I'm sure I was nowhere near as clever and punchy during this piece to camera, but it still made the BBC news.

Then, in 1987 I made a decision to do something that I really wanted to do and I went all out to make it happen. That decision would change the course of my life and lead me to where I am now.

An advert in a newspaper: "Trainee Fingerprint Officer at New Scotland Yard".

Now this I **was** interested in. I had been quite happy in my job at the school and by then I had done well in my exams and was a qualified lab tech, but it wasn't a very cool job.

My friends had cool jobs. Tracey worked at the Cabinet Office, Sally was a research scientist, Alison was climbing the corporate ladder in banking. I just worked in a school lab. This though. Scotland Yard! I had to apply for this. Not just apply for it, I had to get it!

Honestly, at the time I had no real idea what a fingerprint officer did. "The Bill" was on TV, and I had never seen a fingerprint officer on it, yet I was determined to be one and quickly made the decision to apply.

I was so determined to get that job. As a part of the assessment process I took a test for colour blindness and the guy conducting it declared that I was "slightly colour blind". I asked him to show me where I had gone wrong.

I knew I wasn't colour blind.

I used to do this test on the kids at the school, so I knew
the rules. You should only show a few pages. This guy had
made me look at every single page. I pointed his mistake
out to him (how brave was I?). He allowed me to do it
again and declared at the end that I was "ok this time"!

Another great decision.

Had I not gone along with my gut and challenged him,
my chances of being a fingerprint officer may have been
scuppered at the first hurdle.

A week or so later a letter arrived, inviting me for interview. I was so sure I would get the job that I bought a new
jacket to wear for the interview. A friend questioned my
ability to afford the jacket and I said it was ok, I was going
to get the job and have no problems affording it.

I decided to believe the job was mine, before the interview.
I was in no doubt whatsoever that it **was** mine.

Now comes the part where what you take to interview isn't
just your ability to fit into the role you've applied for, but
to show what else you can bring to the party.

Remember that I was a Cub Scout leader? I had only
started helping at the local cub pack when I was a Girl
Guide in order to earn a badge. I didn't know that
gaining that badge would be the start of fifteen years'
service within the Scouting community. Nor did I know
that the member of the panel who asked about my

hobbies and interests was also a Scout Leader. It was a dream interview, and I was offered the job. So, my decision to volunteer and make a lasting commitment to it paid off.

I started working in the Fingerprint Bureau at New Scotland Yard in September 1987. This was a whole new ball game from working in a school. I felt like I had finally left school and was a proper "grown up". Please note that I have since made the decision to never grow up. I think it's far more fun not having to "adult" all the time but have learned how to fake "adulting" when necessary.

My five-minute cycle ride to school had become an hour's commute on foot, train and tube with a 5am alarm call to get me there in time for the 7am start.

Until 2016 New Scotland Yard was on Broadway, Victoria. Two ordinary looking giant towers faced the entrance to St. James tube station. The famous revolving sign emblazoned with "New Scotland Yard" stood in front of them.

You'll know the sign. It's the one that news reporters stand in front of when presenting the news. It was to become the sign I would rush past as fast as I could whenever I saw a boom mike and cameras.

I made conscious efforts not to be filmed or photographed while working for the Police Service. I did once let the BBC film the back of my head and my gloved hands as I examined something, but other than that, I avoided all media.

That first day I met with my fellow newbies as we embarked on the Basic Fingerprint Course. The very first step ahead of five years of training before we would be registered as Fingerprint Experts. From day one I loved it.

I enjoyed getting to know my new workmates and learning a new skill. There was lots to learn and exams to take. No pass meant no job, so I got my head down and got on with it. After around five weeks we had all passed our initial exams and were assigned to teams in the Fingerprint Bureau itself.

This was spread across two floors with the "Main" (SO4) Bureau on one level and the Scenes of Crime department (SO3) on the other. I was sent to a team within the Main Bureau and spent the best part of nine months "coding" fingerprints. It was hugely different then, and people who had been arrested the previous day would have their fingerprints taken onto paper fingerprint forms and the forms sent to us to record and file.

These days the fingers are rolled on a glass plate and the images scanned across to the database which holds all prints from all forces.

Then, we used a filing system named after Sir Edward Henry, a pioneer of fingerprints who set up the Metropolitan Police Fingerprint Bureau in 1901. This filing system used the patterns on each finger; and the "count" of each countable pattern and forms were stacked in "bundles" with a piece of wood top and bottom and held together with a ratchet strap.

Every day, each new fingerprint form had to be "coded" and that code put into the database to see if there was already a set of prints for that person or if it was a brand-new offender. I am sure it will surprise few to hear that we had the fingerprints of many Mickey Mouses and Donald Ducks come into the branch who later turned out to be someone else entirely!

After around nine months working "downstairs", I was moved to up to the seventh floor and onto a "breakers" team. This is where the finger marks lifted from scenes of burglaries, thefts and car crime were sent. We would search through the fingerprint bundles and use the computer systems to search the database to see if they matched the prints of anyone on record.

Throughout my time working in both departments I was undergoing continuous training, and after around three years I took a course that qualified me to examine crime scenes and I was posted to a police station as a SOCO – Scene of Crime Officer. I was fortunate to be posted to a station not far from where I lived, so my hour commute had been cut to just fifteen minutes. I loved the work out "on area". We had a great team at the nick, and I loved getting out and about meeting those who had been victims of crime (I don't believe they are called victims now – injured parties seems to fit the bill these days).

Whilst it is not nice to see people in distress after they have been burgled, injured or had property stolen, I enjoyed finding out what had taken place and piecing together the evidence. Being able to find some evidence to take away, giving a chance of tracking down a suspect and locating items that have been stolen, is priceless.

The world of crime is a tough one to work in, but boy did we have some fun along the way. When dealing with other people's misery on a daily basis it's really important to throw some laughs into the mix too. So, whilst the work side of my policing life was serious and all efforts were made to locate and retrieve evidence that would either prove or disprove someone's involvement in a crime, I also had a lot of fun.

The culture of "work hard, play hard" that existed at the Yard was even more evident now and, as a singleton, it was easy for me to stay at work late if things kicked off and I was needed. Equally, there were many after work drinks that ended in lock ins till the early hours. This is when you really get to know the people you work with and, as a team, we all supported each other through tough times.

I have many great memories of working with police and civilian staff based at several stations across South East

London and remain good friends with many of them to this day. Some of my closest friends are those I met through work. I even married one!

It was being married that took me from London to Suffolk. I'd met my husband whilst on a stint back at the Yard. Whilst being married had never been on my radar of "must dos", when I got to know him it just seemed like the most natural thing to do. We married in 1997 when he was a pupil barrister. He'd loved the social side of working in fingerprints but not the work side, so had studied for a law degree at night school then went on to take his Bar exams before being called to the Bar in 1996.

He found himself a position which meant working away from home, travelling back to me in Surrey on the weekends. This wasn't ideal for us as newlyweds, but it worked only because we knew it was for the short term. So when I saw a vacancy for a qualified SOCO in Suffolk I applied for it and let the Universe take the driving seat.

I had lived in the same area for all my 34 years and had never considered moving away. I loved my job and the prospect of moving up the ranks that came with it; I had a wide circle of friends nearby; I had a lovely flat which was close to the railway station and just a half hour drive from the police station I was posted to at that time.

I had no desire to leave all this, but it wasn't just me now. I had to think of both of us, so when I was selected for the job in Suffolk, I felt that the Universe had answered, and we started making plans to move.

The flat went on the market and we bought a cottage in a tiny Suffolk village. I don't remember having any doubts about it at all. The decision was made, and I just got on with it. My husband started to apply to chambers in Norwich and farewells were made to our London life.

I need to add a sidenote here. I have few regrets in life. I believe the only things we regret are those we don't do rather than those we do, and one of only two regrets I have is that I didn't keep my flat and let it out as a rental. Hindsight is a marvellous thing!

And so it was that in August 1998, I started working for Suffolk Constabulary. This was a different ball game altogether. At the Met I was an Identification Officer covering the role of both Fingerprint Expert and Crime Scene Examiner. Here I was solely a Crime Scene Examiner. I was based at Lowestoft Police Station, the most easterly police station in the country and the SOCO office overlooked the sea.

Lowestoft town has some beautiful buildings, and the beach is amazing. Sadly, it also has high crime and unemployment rates. The upside of this was that it kept me busy.

The SOCO's office was based at Lowestoft because this is where most of the crime we covered occurred, but our area stretched to around 800 square miles, so a lot of driving was involved.

My last postings in the Met had been around the Wandsworth, Tooting, Clapham and Brixton areas where serious crimes occurred daily. Here I was in Suffolk but still with my London mindset. I remember taking a call one day asking me to attend a scene at Southwold. For those who don't know, Southwold is a very genteel coastal town which attracts well to do families for their summer jaunts. Many of the properties are second homes, and the town gets busy in the summer months when "the Londoners" arrive.

I imagined that maybe someone had arrived for the weekend to find they'd been broken into or that a car had had something stolen from it. But no, I was called to look at graffiti on a bus shelter! I had gone from stabbings and rapes with the odd murder thrown in, to graffiti.

It seemed incredible that we were dealing with such minor crimes, but oh, how lovely that I was living in an area where this was taken seriously and that the time, funds and manpower were in place to investigate. I doubt that it is the same now.

Life went on and we settled well into work and enjoyed village life. I worked alternate weekends and was on call a lot, but we had a great social life, getting to know new friends locally and with regular visits from our old friends from London.

A much wanted and loved baby came along in 2001 and I went part time at work. Not a huge decision to have to make as my husband had the potential to earn far more than me, so it was a no brainer for me to take on fewer hours and have more time to be a hands on Mum to baby Max.

In 2006, a serial killer by the name of Stephen Wright showed up in Ipswich.

It was a terrible time during which the bodies of five murdered women were discovered at different locations close to Ipswich. This all took place between 30th October and 10th December and these unprecedented times put an enormous pressure on the relatively small Suffolk Constabulary. Unmanageable without help from other forces, police officers and staff were brought in from across the country to assist Suffolk's officers and to free up some to maintain the normal workload. People do not stop committing crimes when there is a big case on the go, and this still needed to be policed.

The press were camped out at Police Headquarters and Police were working round the clock to identify the killer. The Forensic Science Services had their hands full with huge numbers of scenes to examine and the labs and fingerprint bureau were inundated with evidence to analyse. And so it was I found myself returning to work in a fingerprint bureau and again, it was an easy choice to make. They needed help to compare and identify the thousands of extra finger marks they were receiving on top of the normal workload; I was happy to step in.

I stayed at the Bureau for a couple of years, and during this time I was going through the application process to emigrate to Australia. I had always wanted to live there and after a couple of visits my husband felt the same so we went through all the hoops necessary to make it happen.

This was a HUGE decision to make, but one that I was so certain of that I really didn't have any reservations. My only real gulps came from leaving family and friends behind, but the world is a small place now and I absolutely knew that when I said goodbye to everyone it wouldn't be for the last time.

Little did I know that having sold the house and packed all our belongings into a container I'd be repeating the process for a return journey in just under a year's time.

There is no need to go into details here. Suffice to say, this was a MASSIVE decision to make but one I felt I had little choice over. We came back here but my heart was still in Australia and my husband's heart was with someone else. The decision to go our separate ways needed little discussion and I started my journey on the path to being the "strong independent woman" that others speak of.

I had to accept the whole drama as another stitch in life's tapestry and move on with things to take me forward.

I returned to work in the Fingerprint Bureau in February 2010 and soon started working in the fingerprint lab where chemicals are used to develop finger marks. I loved working there. I had spent some time in the lab whilst working for the Met and of course, all that time I worked in a school lab meant my lab skills were now being used again. It's funny how we call upon skills that we had considered put to bed years previously.

Restructuring meant that Suffolk and Norfolk constabularies were joined in a collaboration which meant that the lab I was working in was mothballed and that Suffolk lab work was to be done in conjunction with Norfolk's at their lab.

For me, this was fantastic. On returning to the UK we had bought a house in Norfolk that is a hop skip and jump away from where the joint lab was to be sited. No more early drives for me, I could just take a quick walk and I would be at work. Perfect.

I enjoyed it for a while, and when Suffolk Fingerprint Bureau was moved to the same location to join up with Norfolk's Bureau it was lovely having the team back together.

By now I had been in the job for nearly thirty years, and whilst years before I had been only too willing to stay late and be at a crime scene for days on end, as a single parent this was no longer possible. I wanted to be at home when school was out. I wanted us to eat together and to ensure homework was being done on time. If I wasn't there, no one would be so when talks of extending the working day started, I became increasingly concerned how this would work for me.

I loved what I did (I'm sure if you were to cut me in half there would be a fingerprint running through me like a stick of Blackpool rock), but I needed to get out before I stopped enjoying it. I had another fifteen years before I could retire, and I wanted to try something else.

I listened to myself from my Akela days. Stop while you're still enjoying it, then you will still love it.

This is exactly what I did. I had done some freelancing, teaching CSI in schools so I took a job with a company on a short term contract. They had an education side to their business but were thinking of closing it down. They took me on to keep it going while they made up their minds. They decided to close it down and so I found myself unemployed. I was 52 and without a job. The only thing I knew was fingerprints and forensics. Who on Earth would employ me?

I hadn't applied for a job nor been for an interview since way back in 1987 when I applied to work at Scotland Yard.

The thought of looking for work didn't appeal so I made a BIG decision. I grew a pair of balls and decided to start my own business.

I rocked up for my first meeting at the job centre and told my "Job Coach" that I wouldn't be on her books for long as I was setting up my own business. I asked to be enrolled on their New Enterprise Allowance Scheme. This was an alternative to Job Seekers Allowance which helped people set up in their own business.

I was the first person she had signed up to this scheme and we muddled our way through it together. I enrolled and met with a fabulous business coach who led me through the initial stages of a making a business plan. Using a tiny amount of injury compensation I had received when a taxi rear ended my car the year before, Forensic Minds was born.

Knowing how many people are interested in fingerprints and forensics I set up my business to deliver fun immersive CSI themed activities so people can learn about it and take on the role of CSI for themselves.

I deliver activities for corporate entertainment, team builds and private parties. I teach educational workshops in schools and colleges, speak, and deliver a range of online events.

My business has gone from strength to strength and I have grown as a person. I tell people that "I'm only an expert in fingerprints and wing everything else" but the truth is, I have gained skills I never would have dreamed of had I stayed where I was.

I have even found myself back in front of the TV cameras as a commentator on crime documentaries.

I don't yet have any regular staff working for me but have an amazing team that I call upon to help when needed. I have built a wide circle of friends in the business world and have learned so much from them. I am still learning. Every day I learn something new, and it's exciting.

I had been looking at the fifteen years that lay ahead before I could retire with dread. Now I look forward to it and think of the amazing places it is going to take me. I have big plans for the future and am looking forward to putting them into practice.

This year has seen the world turn inside out and upside down and inside out. We have all had to adapt and I am grateful that I have been able to do so.

I am not sure I would have had the time to write this were it not for the world slowing down, and this is where I come to my second regret. That I didn't keep a record of all the funny, sad, thought provoking and crazy things that I did when I was working for the Police. I am often asked to write a book on my life of crime. Notes would have made it so much easier. Without them I'm relying on my memory, but it's opening up and I have some good stories coming back to me. So watch this space: a book is on its way.

All this has happened because I remembered back to my Scouting days and stopped while I was still enjoying it and I would encourage others to do the same.

Meanwhile, if I can offer any advice it would be this.

Whenever you have a decision to make, ask yourself three things.

What does your head say?

What does your heart say?

What does your gut say?

I believe that the answers will help you decide.

If my experience is anything to go by, your gut will never let you down. Trust it, thank it and go with it.

Above all, once you think you've had enough of something, you probably have. Walk away before you stop enjoying it.

Quit before it's shit.

ABOUT THE AUTHOR

Diane Ivory

Diane Ivory is a former Scotland Yard Fingerprint Expert and Crime Scene Examiner. After leaving the Police Service after nearly thirty years helping to solve crimes across London, Norfolk and Suffolk, she created her events business Forensic Minds.

Her enthusiasm as she shares her knowledge of the world of fingerprints and forensics is obvious and she delivers her immersive CSI themed events and workshops with great energy and humour.

She has delivered murderous team building events to a variety of clients including AstraZeneca, Suffolk University, Norfolk County Council and Racing Post and taught thousands of inquisitive young minds across the country at countless schools and colleges.

She has also appeared as the Forensic Expert in the TV Crime Documentary Murder By The Sea.

Her mission is to provide something that is inclusive to all and that participants walk away from having had a fabulous time and learnt something they didn't know before.

CONTACT:

EMAIL diane@forensicminds.co.uk
WEBSITE https://forensicminds.co.uk/
FACEBOOK https://www.facebook.com/
groups/236534247430908

facebook.com/ForensicMindsUK

instagram.com/forensicmindsuk

6

EMILY HARRISON

Getting My Shit Together

I am an over-thinker, a constant worrier, and I can be incredibly emotional. Throw into the melting pot of crazy a dreamer, and you get me! Anyone that knows me may not describe those things about me first: they will probably say I am calm, confident and determined – pretty good things to describe and all true, but they aren't fundamentally the first thing that I am, these are the things I want people to think I am. That is my exterior self, my "I have my shit together self," the on the surface impression I give. My "I've got my shit together" mask. No one really needs to see me going over and over the same things, stressing over minute pointless things. I would definitely scare off even my hardened friends.

These conflicting traits and intense emotions make me a handful, and it means I am not everyone's cup of tea. The worrier in me hates this and struggles with this notion.

The reason I have all of these traits and why I actually like to keep all my shit to myself and keep it all together is that I am a people pleaser.

There, I have said it: I love to make others happy. Before I addressed and became aware of it all, I used to only feel happy when others around me were happy WITH me, that their impression of me was good. How messed up is that? These over-thinking, over-worrying, dreamer and emotional traits have been formed from years of trying to make others happy before myself. From worrying… no, agonizing… over what people think of me, how I should be in order for others to like me, to be proud of me, to even want to be my friend, love me or even just accept me.

This people pleasing need made me ignore myself and meant at times I lost who I was and stumbled down paths that I thought would mean others would be happier with me and like me more. I learnt how to adjust to make them happier with me, to be more like them, to change for them. I was a fake version of myself. For years my life was like this, from primary school, in fact.

When I realised that having my shit together for others, making others happy, being how others wanted me to be, was in fact destroying any chance of me having an ounce of contentment, that was the massive turning point. It was a slap you round the face moment.

But this slap was needed, and now I can honestly say it was the best thing that happened to me.

I can now say that I am a people pleasing person who now knows when to please myself before others, when to keep my shit together and when to let it all come out.

I have channelled this need to make others happy into an incredibly successful business and it makes me so much more aware of my customers' experiences and their journey with the company. Because I am so much more aware of it, I am more careful with who I try to please, I keep my shit together more and fundamentally I can say that, yes, I bloody love my life and what I do now, even if I dare say bollocks to those that aren't happy with me.

I now use these traits and see them as a positive thing that enhances my life. I am not ashamed of them and they aren't like a dirty secret that I have to hide. I embrace them fully, I make sure I am aware of them and use them for good. They allow me to be a REALLY good people pleaser to those that deserve it! Like my husband, my children, my family, friends, my customers and my staff.

WHERE IT ALL BEGAN; WHEN THE PLEASING STARTED...

Childhood experiences shape your whole mindset – your coping strategies and your general beliefs about the world. My childhood was not a comfortable time. I was always the odd one out, with a different accent, different clothes, or just started school when everyone else had formed friendships. I didn't really have true friends. When I thought I had, I found they were talking about me. Even in primary school, I was chased to the toilets and threatened with a punch or a kick. I spent a lot of time at the bottom of the fields or with the rabbits "cleaning and feeding them" away from other children.

Slowly I would form friendships with others, but I was so wary and so unsure. I created versions of myself that were never true. I created fantasies, untrue life experiences as I felt I had nothing else to talk about or didn't want to talk about the reality, for fear they would think it too dull. I even made up that I had a big brother, as I thought that would stop them picking on me. What I learned was people can be mean and heartless. If you didn't fit in, you were worthless and ignored, or worse still, picked on. Because I was told I was different and felt different, I couldn't find a way of belonging or feeling happy. This was the start of being convinced that the only way to be happy was for others to like me.

Not ever being accepted for who you are as a little girl is bloody hard. To question why you aren't good enough at such a young age scars you. It was the start of me pretending that all was fine. It was the start of wearing my "I have my shit together mask" because for anyone that can remember school, if you showed how upset you were that was even worse.

When I was fourteen, our family moved to the Lake District. An ideal setting for some, but a few years that were hell for me. This was the start of my self-destruction and losing who I was completely. I found nothing I said or did was liked; nothing about me was accepted. At fourteen, I already found the world an incredibly difficult place. After months of endless digs, jokes about me, being chased and fire hoses being turned on as I ran down corridors, or even just not having lunch because of certain prefects on the canteen doors, I was done with life being so cruel. I was hurting.

This was when the first coping strategy for dealing with these thoughts, worries, and emotions came out. I started self-harming. I felt so full of these negative thoughts, I needed to release them. I felt stuck and unable to cope. My parents were busy, and I was angry and sad all at the same time. So I released it. I began cutting myself. It became very addictive, and I was all in.

I would spend most of the day with a mask on, pretending to be someone, longing to be alone, and to release the pain from the day. My play it cool, keep your shit together mask has evolved from this one.

I also found another way to deal with bullies and my life at school. I targeted the ones that hated me, sat next to them, acted like them. I became like them and slowly was accepted by them. It was actually effortless to do, as I was already angry and hurt, so I could quite happily emulate being a bitch outwardly. I was doing this at home already.

So I survived; I just followed suit. All the while, I fanta-sised about what real life would be like. I convinced myself the real world would be juster, fairer, and a much happier place to be.

One day I would stop hurting, one day I wouldn't need to hurt myself to release these feelings, one day I would have something else to make these emotions go away. How bloody wrong was I?

One day I met a boy. He allowed me to fully express my emotional side, so much so he became an obsession. I stopped self-harming and focused everything onto him. I fell deeply in love. I had an outlet for all this emotion, another obsession. The sadness went and was replaced with infatuation and desire. The love was intoxicating. An obsession and a need to be around someone, he became my escape from the world, my drug, my focus, and nothing else mattered.

My world became all about him. No one else mattered as long as he was happy, then I felt as though I was happy. When he ended things after three years, just as I was about to do my A-levels, and then started seeing one of my sister's best friends, you can imagine what that did to me. I stopped caring about anything, nothing really mattered, and I started ignoring all of the warning signs and went deep into self-sabotage and made some bad and weird decisions. I ignored my gut feelings, my life choices were horrendous, and I just switched off from life, responsibilities, and caring.

Moving to University and halls of residence in Sheffield gave me a newfound sense of freedom and, for a while, a time to breathe and start to enjoy myself a little. I had escaped the emotional turmoil, the heartache, and the "friends" I had formed. For a short time, I felt myself. My mask was worn less, and I made some friends who actually liked me. I didn't need to please them for them to like me. It was a really novel feeling.

My first year at university was hedonistic, ridiculous, embarrassing, and very funny. I made bad decisions (but not dangerous ones), made mistakes, spent my student loan far too quickly, but I was happy for the first time ever, not reliant on someone else to make me feel like that, but because I was just having fun.

I fondly look back over that time when life was quite simple. The only worry was how long the queue was at the Leadmill and if you would make it in before you wet yourself. I, of course, failed quite a few times with that task.

Then came the reality: graduation; job responsibilities; LIFE. I thought I had it set. I'd bought a house in my second year, so I was secure. I got a job halfway through my final year, ready for when I finished uni. I was all set for the big wide world. I was all for this incredible journey. I was about to experience what was expected of me and what I expected of life.

Because I felt safe at university, when the safety net left and my uni friends moved away and I was on my own again, the reality of life and my people pleasing need came out. Hello, needy old friend, long time no see!

I started a job in Leeds (a two hour round commute) for the national probation service, managing caseloads of offenders on community support and running group programmes for drink driving offences. It was brilliant first job straight out of uni, but in hindsight a bad move. It made me see life in a very sad, twisted way. If I wasn't already a little despondent with how people treat each other, meeting those who have had to go through the criminal justice system really opened my eyes! Working or serving at Her Majesty's pleasure meant I saw sadness, lack of options and a general depressing view of life on a daily basis.

Everyone was very impressed I had landed this amazing "opportunity". But this opportunity wasn't a particularly fun job and many of my working colleagues were desperately unhappy, unsatisfied and underwhelmed with life and their existence. No chance of pleasing people here. So I stuck my mask on and got on with it. I tried to find something else, something more than just this bloody job!

Surely there could be more, surely there was someone I could focus on and please. I was desperate, needy and vulnerable. I guess I had 'absolute sap' written across my forehead and I got sucked in well and truly. Knowing that I wanted to just make others happy, my next biggest mistake would be a work colleague. Let's call him Ned. Short for knobhead.

One year into the job I met Ned. I fancied him and created an ideal of what he was going to be like as a human being. Sadly, my ideal was far from the reality. I became stuck in this mentally controlling and very destructive relationship. My closest friends were watching. I could see they were concerned but unsure about how to help.

Then after another day of being controlled, manipulated, and threatened yet again, my body and my mind snapped. I had had enough.

A shift had happened in my belief about myself. For one of the first times in my life I stood up for myself. I was finally fed up with pleasing him and pretending to be what he wanted me to be. I left and this then made me feel a new sense of achievement I had never felt before. I felt badass and FREE! This was one of the first times I didn't care what someone thought of me. I had spent so long trying to make him love me, but I realised I didn't want him to, I didn't want to anymore.

I also secured a job closer to home and enjoyed living again. This sense of freedom allowed me to express who I was a bit more and like University I formed more friendships again and I met my now husband. Tim is my nice, calm husband. He doesn't demand anything from me, is emotionally mature and doesn't need me to be anything other than me. He is and always will be my constant. He is my lighthouse through my stormiest moments, and although at times I want to throttle him, he is good for me.

WHEN THE SHIT HITS THE FAN

My current job was the same role with different people, with the same disdain for it as previous colleagues. No difference was being made, no one was leaving happy and I was deeply unfulfilled. There was no one to impress, no one to please, no one to make happy and more fulfilled. So I went searching for something else. I secured a new job, a pilot scheme designed to keep pre-sentenced offenders out of prison and address some of the reasons they found themselves going through the court system.

In theory, this was an incredible opportunity, rewarding, and a meaningful role. I actually thought I might not actually need my "I have my shit together mask" because for once maybe I would actually in real life have it together. The flaw in this whole project came and slapped us all in the face very, very quickly. Most of the "clients" we were "helping" were all innocent! (according to them, of course) Victims of the system apparently, so our hands were tied. We couldn't actually tackle the huge elephant in the room. Their offence. The whole sodding reason they were in front of us. Instead, we had to skirt around it and look at other issues with little powers.

The caseload spiralled from a maximum of ten medium risk cases to over forty with 20+ high risk. It was a disaster. My gut was screaming at me to get out, and my worrier was pulling their hair out at me for not listening. Something was going to go wrong, and very wrong it did.

One of our clients committed suicide in our bail house. Another tried to attack their neighbour with a machete. Another had been living with the victim of his offence the whole time we were "supporting him" and we had missed it. Of *course* we missed it. My housing officer and I were fighting fires with plastic fire engines and watering cans. It was a mess, a complete and utter mess.

New Year's Eve and I had the police calling me because one of my bailees was on the rooftop of his block of flats, naked, threatening to jump unless he spoke to me. Before handing the phone over, the policeman said, "What on earth are you doing? As it clearly isn't working." I don't know, Officer, I don't bloody know. On top of all that, my Grandad was gravely ill, and I was refused leave to go and see him because said bloke with machete needed moving to another house, and the naked flat jumper was demanding to see me for the fifteenth bloody time that week. So Grandad Bill passed away. I didn't get to see him. It was the final straw that not only broke the camel but a whole herd (is it a herd?) of camels.

My innate need to make others happy was sapping me fully as I was focusing on the wrong people AGAIN. I was drained. I was done.

The next few days/weeks were a blur. I was overstressed, over-emotional, and I broke mentally. I walked into work one day and couldn't open a file. I couldn't talk. All I did was cry and shake. My housing support officer took me to the doctors, who immediately signed me off and gave me some very, very strong sleeping and anti-anxiety tablets to calm me down.

I then spent days, weeks, and months, still. Not moving. Flat. I didn't feel like I was getting anything from my life. It felt like existence and a struggle to feel much, except stress, anxiety, and pain. I had done all the right things, ticked the boxes laid out in front of me, did uni, did the house, made the career, the marriage. I continually tried to make others around me happy, proud and worthy and feel better about themselves. Yet I couldn't feel anything except sadness. It was like I saw it all in grey. Tim tried desperately, with little acts of kindness, love, and compassion, but they weren't getting through. All I could feel was the pain. I ached from being so sad every day. Nothing excited me. I was nearing the end of what my body, heart, and soul could take, and I had given up.

There came the choice. The choice to end all of it. I was done with living and ready to give in to nothing. Feeling nothing and no longer worrying.

I had planned it so well. The choice to end my life felt like the easiest decision in the world. I was doing it in the shower with the water running, so there was no mess. My husband always moaned at me for being messy, so I thought that was the kindest thing. As I was starting my plan, and slowly, secretly starting to execute it, in my head I was saying goodbye to people. I ached for the silence.

Tim saw a change in me, knew something wasn't right and made me go with him to his mum's, where she made me talk. I obviously said something that didn't sound quite right because I wasn't allowed out of anyone's sight. Then came the Crisis team meeting and the discussion over being sectioned. This floored me. I had no idea I was outwardly displaying my sadness and hate of being in the world. I then saw how much sadness I was putting onto others. I felt so ashamed that I had felt like this and had ignored others around me and their feelings. That was the start of the turning point for me.

The need to please people around me, the wrong people, meant I was ignoring myself, my husband and my family and friends who all loved me.

GETTING MY SHIT TOGETHER

The realisation that my living a life of expectation and desperately wanting others to be happy with me had led to that dark path, switched my focus.

I realised that I needed to stop fighting against how I am feeling, but to embrace who I am and use what I am to my strengths.

I realised I am GOOD at making people happy, but I need to keep that in check, focusing and using it in the right way, and to allow my over thinker and over worrier time and utilise them properly. I realised that I needed to be my own boss, not because I wasn't good at being employed, but I realised I wanted to create something that was inspiring and create a business that was built on making people happy – to make everyone involved in the business feel valued, accepted and worthy. So I started Emily Bridalwear. This business is built on my traits. It needs me to be emotional when I make decisions, it needs me to overthink and worry in order to make sure I am doing the right thing. It needs me to be a people pleaser to be able to provide the best experience.

It needs me to have my actual shit together.

What this business has done is to allow me to be proud of my traits, proud of my need to make others happy before myself. I have created an ethos within my company that allows my employees to feel the same, to be fully accepted and loved for who they are fully. I have been able to fully express myself in such a way that now makes me proud to be a selective people pleaser.

I have created somewhere that I truly feel like I belong. I feel accepted and fulfilled. By creating a world that is all about acceptance, love and support, my world no longer makes me sad or bitter. That weird, intense, odd one out has finally found her place in life, and I bloody love it.

For anyone still looking for theirs, everything that we have learned in our past is exactly that: previous ways. Being and feeling stuck in yourself is the most terrifying feeling in the world. The only way to free yourself is to know that only you have the power to do it. To truly accept yourself and ALL your traits is the first step, and the first move forward. Finding something that allows you to fully express yourself is part of that journey, part of feeling fulfilled.

You have more strength and capabilities to re-write, channel, and move forward to express who you really are, find what sets your soul on fire, and create real and satisfying contentment. Now THAT is a world I am sure you want to be part of.

Emily Harrison is a multi award winning business owner, running a six figure wedding dress shop in South York-shire. The business is built around strong values and with an unrivalled customer centred approach. She is now on a mission to help other creative women build and adjust their businesses to shift in line with their own values and morals. She is passionate about businesses with a heart and a soul and about giving women the confidence to move away from stagnant business models to a much more altruistic approach that is rewarding in so many different ways, to fundamentally serve the lifeblood of their business, the customer, in a way that is not only beneficial to the success of the business but will in turn provide a fundamental satisfaction that has never been felt before.

With a psychology degree, a diploma in Customer Experience, and years of running and proving her approach works, she is now helping others to achieve the same results.

Emily is sharing her thirteen years of customer focused business knowledge and experience with like minded women who know there is more to running a business than profit and loss sheets and ok service.

CONTACT:

Email: emily@themeasureup.co.uk
Website: www.themeasureup.co.uk

facebook.com/themeasureup
instagram.com/themeasureup

EMMA ROSCOE

NO HOLDS BARRED

"And she always had a way with her brokenness.

She would take her pieces and make them beautiful".

— R.M. DRAKE

I used to be too scared to stand up for what I believed in, to let my vulnerabilities be seen, or to allow my voice to be heard.

Not. Any. More.

For years I felt weak and powerless. And based my self-worth on the validation, or lack of it, I received from others (mostly men). I had spent most of my life silently seeking permission to be myself. Until one day, somewhere in my mid-late thirties, I found myself saying, "Fuck this! I did not survive my trauma just to spend the rest of my life being defined and held back by it."

Please don't get me wrong, I don't throw profanities around like they're confetti, but I refuse to shy away from being real either. Because shit happens. To all of us. And five years ago, I decided to start owning mine in all its fabulously messy glory and take that first fumbling, wobbly step towards becoming the woman I am today. Life chose to make me strong. And I always had the power to decide how I was going to respond to that calling, it just took me twenty years of struggling to find the courage to answer.

Now, whenever I'm about to walk out onto a stage, I harness every ounce of the bravery I showed myself that day and carry it with me. When I speak to an audience, my voice is steady, and my head is held high. In stepping up for myself, not just that day, but on every single day that followed, I was able to connect to my purpose and use the most challenging moments of my life to help others. My vulnerability became my superpower and my bumpy road to self-recovery inspired a survival guide for the women I now mentor.

It all began with my decision to take personal responsibility and to choose bravery over shame, and what followed was a commitment to make that choice over and over again. My success was always within my reach, and yours is no different. You too can choose to stand in your power and proudly own all that you are. Because your success is waiting to be created as soon as you're ready to find the courage to pursue it.

So today, I will share my truth with you. Unapologetically. No holds barred.

THE ROAR

I was screaming. I could feel this primitive roar burning inside my chest, ready to tear my throat open and deafen everyone around me - and yet I was silent. And counting. Because maybe if I concentrated hard enough on working out whether there were 42 or 43 circles on the metal wall art opposite me, I could pretend that I wasn't waiting to hear whether my baby boy was alive or dead. If I closed my eyes hard enough, maybe when I opened them he would still be in my arms and everything would be ok. I could smell him on my pyjama top. I could feel the pain from my c-section wound and the throb of my breasts that were filling with milk to sustain him. But he wasn't with me. He was fighting for his life surrounded by strangers and I just had to sit there and wait - helpless, powerless, terrified.

Even as a little girl, I dreamt of being a Mum. And then, in my early thirties, there was a time when I began to allow myself to believe that it might never happen. But the disappointment of every negative pregnancy test, the heartbreak of every miscarriage, and every single anxious thought and fear I'd had about not being able to sustain this pregnancy either, had all dissolved in a tidal wave of sheer bliss earlier one morning as I sat in my hospital bed with our beautiful boy lying asleep on my chest. I had given birth via an emergency Caesarean two nights prior, but it was in the morning of that day I first wholeheartedly felt like a Mother. He was everything I had ever wished for and more, and I took a picture of us on my phone to try and capture this moment forever.

But just twelve hours after that picture was taken, I found myself sitting in one of those rooms that family members get shown to in hospital dramas, right before a sympathetic-faced doctor comes and tells them that they are very sorry, but there is nothing more they could do. I glanced over to the small table at the side of the room and noticed a Bible on it, and silently started praying to a God that I didn't even believe in.

38, 39, 40… And I was still counting those shitty coloured circles because I dared not look at either John or my Mum through fear of shattering into a million pieces there and then. I just sat there, praying, counting, and desperately clutching on to a cup of tea that had gone cold. I used to think that a good cuppa could make anything more bearable. I was wrong. I also used to think that showing my vulnerability made me weak. And I could not have been more wrong about that either.

As I write this now, I am looking at that moment. My perfect moment. Captured forever in the photo I took of us both, framed, and sat proudly on the windowsill above my desk. And next to it a collage he made me at nursery three years later.

WARRIORS

Nothing could have prepared me for the trauma of that night. Or for watching our baby sedated and covered in wires and intravenous drips whilst a machine breathed air into his tiny lungs. I could barely cope with looking at him, and not being able to hold him was excruciating. But we had created a little fighter and he fought hard. Later the following day, the senior neonatal nurse couldn't hide her smile as she told us how he had tightly gripped his own respiration tube and pulled it out as his sedation wore off. "My little warrior," I thought.

An intraventricular bleed on his brain had almost stolen him away at just three days of age. But he was still here, I was finally a Mum, and I was so, so lucky. I became hell-bent on making sure I savoured every precious second. This was all I had ever wanted, and I was going to be happy. No matter what.

So, when we finally got to take him home, I packed up my trauma in my hospital bag and added it to all the other emotional baggage I had accumulated and carried with me since I was fifteen. Over the years I had perfected the art of sucking up my pain, pushing it down, and burying it deep until it became second nature. It was my go-to coping mechanism.

I didn't want to be seen as damaged or broken, because broken things got thrown away and I believed my damage made me hard to love. But little did I know that those same broken pieces and vulnerabilities would one day be my superpower. And that I was soon to become a warrior too.

MIXTAPES

I'm going to take you back to 1996. Just for a moment. This was the year the Spice Girls first entered the charts with 'Wannabe' and Take That released their Greatest Hits album. I, however, was more into alternative/indie rock, dance music, and figuring out who and what I wanted to be. Through risk of making myself sound cooler than I was though, you should probably also know that I was a good student, only ever had one after-school detention, and whilst I had friends, I definitely wasn't one of the popular girls we all remember from school. 1996 was also the year something happened to me that changed the trajectory of my life.

I was fifteen years old and living my 90's fashion best life, wearing the Levi 501s I had begged my parents to get me for my birthday, along with a black puffa jacket. To top it off I was also rocking a big, permed hair and Heather Shimmer lipstick combo! Life was good. A group of us girls were spending the night together at a friend's. We jumped off the bus and were busy chatting as we made our way across to her house.

And then it hit me.

A Peugeot 205 on a 60 mile per hour road.

I don't remember the car striking me, my body smashing the windscreen, or biting through my own chin on impact. I'm not sure at what point I lost consciousness or when I fully regained it. I can't recall ricocheting down the road on my back when the car stopped moving. But I know I still have tiny pieces of the grit from that road in the scars I've been left with. My whole stay in hospital has always remained a hazy blur and my strongest memory from that time are the two mixtapes my friend made for me by recording tracks off the radio. I listened to them on my Walkman every day throughout my recovery and allowed myself to get lost in the music, because it was easier than facing up to what had happened to me.

I would like to take this opportunity to throw some more love on the epicness that was 90's fashion. A doctor informed me and my parents that it was my puffa jacket flying up behind my head as I bounced down the road that saved my life. My back looked horrific, but I was still alive, and so I counted myself lucky.

I missed quite a bit of school whilst I recovered and, to begin with, had to return in a wheelchair. On my first day back, a boy stood in front of me blocking my exit. He looked me up and down, kissed his lips at me, sniggered, and said, "Well at least your face didn't get too fucked up." He walked away with his mates laughing and I just sat there, wishing I could disappear.

Those few words were all it took for me to start believing that my worth was largely dependent on my looks and what other people thought of me.

I revised for and sat my mock exams for my GCSEs whilst recovering. My results were bad and I wouldn't get offered a place at the sixth form college I wanted to attend with those grades, so my teachers for the core subjects had to write letters to 'vouch' for my academic abilities. I had to ask for validation that I was 'good enough' from other people. And that, that was the first time I felt like I wasn't enough. I began to see myself with very different eyes and my self-esteem had taken a severe battering. But I didn't talk about any of this. I just sucked it up, pushed it down, kept smiling, and carried on. Remember that go-to coping mechanism I told you about? Well, this is when it started, along with me devaluing myself.

If I could write fifteen year old Emma a letter, I would tell her that she always had been, and always would be more than enough. And that speaking out about our feelings, insecurities and struggles is not a sign of weakness, but one of true strength. I used to believe that carrying on regardless and pretending that things hadn't caused me emotional harm was brave. But I now know that it was a seriously misguided choice and a damaging way to treat myself.

Less than a year later, I fell for the wrong boy and became a teenage girl in an emotionally abusive, controlling, and sexually coercive relationship.

STICKS & STONES

Ten years passed before I found the courage to leave him. I spent a whole decade of my life accepting the love I thought I deserved, and for much of that time even being grateful for it. My experiences within that relationship affected and shaped me in so many ways and over time became my new normal. I internalised all the shame and blame and guilt and put it all on me. I carried that shit around with me everywhere I went whilst hiding it away from everyone around me and the outside world. My game face was in a league of its own, and some of my 'everything is ok and I'm fine' performances were Oscar-worthy. It was exhausting, and my mental health severely paid the price for it. More than once. But those same experiences, and the choices I made, showed me how strong and determined I could be. My personal resilience came into its own. Upon reflection, that relationship taught me so much about myself - how much I could endure and overcome. But perhaps most importantly, it showed me what love is not, and what it never should be, and that I deserved so much better.

I studied Criminology and Law at University, and for my dissertation, I chose to do a case study and literature review about women who had killed their violent and abusive partners. I spent months researching the cases of female victims of intimate partner abuse and never made the connection to myself or my own experiences. Not even once. I was in total denial about my own circumstances, so much so that I stayed in that relationship for another five years before I saved myself.

I learned the phrase 'Sticks and stones may break my bones, but words will never hurt me,' when I was a child. But by the age of 26, the words and behaviours of a man who claimed to love me had driven me to a mental place where I actually wanted the stick. I even started deliberately pushing him for it. I needed him to throw the stones because I believed that if he physically hurt me, I would have no excuse to stay. Someone would be able to see what he had done. The harm would be visible for once. If he hit me, they would make me leave him and it would stop. It would all stop.

I still feel sick admitting that I longed for him to hurt me in that way, but remembering how inadequate I felt in being able to save myself is the reason I share it, and I'm not ashamed anymore. It is far easier not to tell a difficult story. To never shine a light on your rawest feelings, never find the strength to share your darkest times. But I think it's important that we do. When we don't talk about difficult experiences and painful memories – and instead, keep them buried deep within us – we allow them a power they don't deserve. And when we let the shit we have experienced define us, we become disconnected from our own innate power and our true selves. I spent far too many years living like that.

Allowing ourselves to embrace our vulnerabilities, lower our emotional barricades, and let out all our unspoken words, can set us free. There is so much power in our truths, and we can own it all, if we choose to. I first allowed myself to talk about mine in a doctor's office when I asked for help. And later in a coaching session when I spoke of my true feelings about myself. Over time I became comfortable enough to share some of them over coffee with friends. I learnt through experience that speaking our truth can be instrumental in reconnecting us to our power. So much so that in September 2019 I stepped out onto a TEDx stage and shone a spotlight on some of the traumas and feelings I'd sucked up, pushed down and buried deep over the years. Not only did I get to own every single word I shared that day, without shame or apology, but I was also able to permanently extinguish the last flickers of power those same experiences had held over me for two decades of my life.

UNRECOGNISABLE

I did it very politely, and my delivery was kind. Not because that's what he deserved, but because I didn't have any fight left in me. I just needed to save myself as quietly as I could, because I was so very tired. Tired of maintaining the façade of a normal relationship. Tired of pretending to still love him. But mostly I was tired of looking at myself in the mirror every day and barely recognising the broken, desperate woman staring back at me. Silently pleading with me to make it stop. To make it all stop. I did not want to be her anymore. At the time I felt so weak, but I now see it all with very different eyes. I know how much courage it took to decide to leave him in the way I did. In fact, to leave him, full stop. I didn't want to make a scene, I just needed it to be over. And the truth is, when it comes to ending a toxic relationship, leaving is the bravest thing you will ever do. And the safer you can do that, the better. You take all the strength that's enabled you to survive up to this point and you use it to carry yourself out of the door – for the last time.

As I handed him back the engagement ring I had been wearing for the past seven years, my hands were shaking. My heart was pounding so hard I thought it could burst through my chest any second and I felt like I was going to throw up, but I still let him hold me that one last time. Not to be kind. Not to spare his feelings. Not because it's what he deserved but because even at the moment I was leaving him I still felt like I was under his control. I so desperately needed to just slip away out of his life as quietly as I could.

When I fell in love at the age of sixteen, I was hoping for a fairy tale. And I believed every "Sorry" and every declaration of love and adoration that fell from his lips. But I learned the very hard way, that an apology without change is just pure manipulation. Something I became very well accustomed to. When I finally walked away all those years later, I was left with emotional scars, the most brutal self-talk you could imagine, and destroyed self-worth.

Emotional abuse is so complex, and the wounds and harm caused are invisible to the naked eye. But if I could have worn mine on my skin, I would have been unrecognisable. And yet there I was, still standing, still smiling, and moving forward one tiny step at a time, navigating my way through moment by moment, day by day. In all honesty, surviving shit takes guts and in those early days, there was very little glory to behold. But it did get easier, and less painful, and I promise you that eventually the faint light at the end of the tunnel starts to get brighter, and closer. Until one day you look at yourself in the mirror and start to feel love and respect for the woman looking back at you. I walked away from that relationship feeling completely broken, but I was eventually able to take those pieces of myself and turn them into something beautiful.

MY TURN

My journey into motherhood and what happened with my son Logan when he was still tiny, had a devastating impact on me. I turned to my usual coping mechanism of sucking it up, pushing it down, and burying it deep, and added it to all the unresolved trauma from my abusive relationship and my accident. I was confident that if I crammed it into my suitcase of emotional shit and sat on top of it, I'd still be able to get the zip done up and none of it would start spilling out. Because a bit more wouldn't hurt, right?

As the days and weeks passed after bringing him home, I began to realise how wrong I was. I relived those terrifying scenes from the hospital over and over again, both in my dreams and when I was awake. My mental health was slipping through my fingers once more, and I felt like I was drowning.

I was so, so lucky to still have him, and yet I continued to torture myself with my thoughts. I knew something had to change. But I did not wake up one morning and realise I didn't want to feel this way anymore. I woke up every morning feeling like that, day after day, for months on end. And then one afternoon I was sat on the sofa with Logan stretched out on my lap. As I cradled his head in my hands, I looked deep into his beautiful brown eyes and cried. This tiny person was depending on me. He had already come through so much and deserved the best Mummy he could have. But as things were, I wasn't capable of being her, and certainly not if I continued to deteriorate. So, I decided to step up, not because I believed I was worth it, but because I knew without a shadow of a doubt that Logan was. He had been so brave and fought so hard, and now it was my turn.

It would have been easy to carry on struggling because it felt safely familiar to me. I had walked that walk before, but this time I could feel, deep inside, a 'knowing' that I had to call time out. The thought of spending the rest of my life feeling this way was becoming too much to bear. It was make or break time. But there was no cross-roads to be reached and stood at, because the metaphorical clichés we hear about are not a pre-requisite of deciding to step up for yourself. We all have the power within us to choose at any given moment. This moment was mine to own and when your time comes you will know too.

I didn't do it all on my own. I was prescribed medication again, and needed counselling and coaching, but ultimately it started and ended with me, because whilst none of my trauma was my fault, my healing was 100% my responsibility. Nobody was going to come and save me, least of all from myself. Taking personal accountability for my thoughts, my feelings, and the choices I made every single day was the most empowering thing I ever did for myself. It put me back in the driving seat of my own life.

But to be able to start moving forward, I had to take off my mask; the one I had been wearing and relying on for so long that it had become my second skin. It left me vulnerable as fuck, but it was so very needed if I was ever going to find my way out and to the other side. I gave myself permission to feel, to forgive, and start letting go. I owed myself a million apologies for putting up with and allowing shit that I never deserved. And as hard as it was to do, forgiving myself was a transformational part of my recovery and reconnection.

Now when I look in the mirror, I feel damn proud of the woman staring back at me. I know where she's been, what she's experienced, and how those things left her feeling about herself. I've shared her joy and endured her pain. I know how many times she felt like quitting. I know about every single time she doubted herself. I've heard all her negative self-talk (and it was brutal). But now, when I look into the eyes that were once so lost and desperate, I see only passion, kindness, and determination with a cheeky glint of badass.

She is a perfect blend of grit and grace and owning all that she is. And I love her for it.

Something beautiful emerged from everything I experienced, and it was ME.

QUEEN

I was hiding down one of the Christmas decorations aisles in B&M when it happened.

It's certainly not the setting I'd have chosen for an epiphany, but sometimes these things catch you by surprise! I had made a dive for the nearest aisle after realising the woman in front of me at checkout five was the mother of my abusive ex. A second later I recoiled in panic as my eyes confirmed that the man standing with her was him. Twelve years had passed since the day I walked away and yet here I was, adrenaline coursing through my body and a visceral reaction to get myself out of there as quickly as I could. He hadn't seen me, there was no threat, but I was reeling. I had been out of that relationship for longer than the decade I stayed in it for, but at that moment, I felt like I was right back in the thick of it. I was panicked. I ran. And then, moments later, as I brushed the glitter off myself and straightened my coat after climbing out of a Christmas display, it hit me, the realisation that I had a choice.

The reality was that I couldn't go back and erase any of the shit I had experienced in that relationship, or deny the emotionally damaged legacy it left me with, but I could absolutely choose how I handled seeing him again after all these years and I could choose how I moved forward with the rest of my life. And at that moment, I remembered who hell I was, what I'd already overcome, and that my past didn't get to shame me or emotionally batter me anymore - not today, not tomorrow, and as sure as hell not in B&M of all places!

And with that, I made my way back to the tills with my head held high and paid for my loo rolls and dog treats. Like a Queen (well sort of!).

Later on, when I was curled up on the sofa with a cuppa, I kept finding glitter stuck to me. I smiled as I removed each one of those tiny sparkles because what had happened earlier was powerful. The Universe had tested me, and I had stepped up. And then, I knew. I had no idea what it would look like, or how I was going to do it, but I knew there and then, that I wanted to help other women who had survived intimate partner abuse reconnect to their personal power, and to not be held back by the aftermath of their experiences, so they too could be free to live the rest of their lives on their own terms.

The uncomfortable truth is that our past experiences will always be a part of us. But our broken pieces are not anything to be ashamed of and they do not get to choose who we are today or who we become. We do. Don't get me wrong, some days I still look back, but only to appreciate how far I've come, because I didn't survive all that shit just to spend the rest of my life being defined by it. And if any of my story resonates with you, please know you don't have to either.

We get to choose.

THE ROAR

I still have it. But my roar is no longer a fiery ball of primitive pain ready to tear me open. These days it is a passion that burns deep inside of me. Something that I found once I was able to heal and reconnect to my own power. And something that I finally understood as I picked those tiny specks of glitter off myself. I made a promise to start showing up for me, as my true self and make zero apologies for it.

And so today, as the woman I am, with a little more becoming still to do, I fully embrace my roar so I can show the world exactly who the real Emma Roscoe is.

I choose to own my shit and love myself fiercely for it.

Because I know surviving really can be beautiful.

ABOUT THE AUTHOR

Emma Roscoe

Emma Roscoe is a passion driven advocate, mentor, and speaker on a mission to show how surviving can be beautiful and lighting the way for women who have experienced intimate partner abuse to reconnect to their personal power. Having previously spent twenty years of her life shrouded in shame by her past traumas and experiences, she now empowers other women to start owning their shit, without being defined or held back it anymore, so they are free to live life on their own terms... whatever that means to them personally.

As an inspirational and motivational speaker, she has spoken on stages including TEDx, sharing her journey and message of how taking personal responsibility for your own healing can change your life. Regardless of what happens to us, we get to choose how we respond.

CONTACT:

Email: emma@kintsugicollective.org.uk
Website: www.kintsugicollective.org.uk

f facebook.com/TheKintsugiCollective
📷 instagram.com/the_kintsugicollective

HAYLEY JONES

CHOOSE TO RISE UP AND BE STRONG

WHAT HAD I BECOME?

As I opened my eyes, I just felt so groggy and spaced out. I tried to sit up but couldn't quite make it into the sitting position. I could hear crying from my little boy who was sixteen months, and my two-and-a-half-year-old daughter was asking for Mummy. Dan was busy cooking in the kitchen.

I remember at this point, thinking, is this it for me?

It was an all-time low. The feelings of shame, guilt and hatred I felt were so strong, it consumed my being every day. I felt my life was pointless and void of anything. The medication had turned me into a zombie. I didn't want to be around people, even my own family and the pain inside my body was excruciating, even with medication.

As Dan walked into the room juggling plates, I looked over at the washing he had folded, the room he had cleaned (well, to a man's standard at least) and the shame hit me again.

My head hurt so badly, so I staggered upstairs to lay on the bed, put a pillow over my face and screamed into it so loudly I thought my eyeballs would pop out. Enough was enough.

I was at another crossroads in my life. I had two choices. Either I just learn to live like this, listen to all the expert's medical advice, live with medication as a daily routine, don't work another day of my life, transform our house to enable me to get around and just learn to live with the crippling pain OR take back control.

I remember thinking of my favourite childhood film, *Labyrinth* when Sarah says, 'You have no power over me,' words that fuelled me and still do. I needed to take back control of my life and my destiny. I'd worked so hard to get where I was up until that tragic day when my world disappeared before me, but in that moment, I had to choose between feeling sorry for myself and becoming a person I didn't even recognise in the mirror, or I could get up and fight, for myself, for my daughter D'Arcy, my son Harrison and my partner, now husband, Dan. I wanted the old Hayley back, warts and all and I decided at that moment that's what I would do.

THE EARLY YEARS

I was born in Birmingham, and I had two younger sisters. I was always the bossy one. Of course, that's what big sisters do. I was also the protector although they didn't realise this until they were much older. Home life had its good but also quite a lot of bad. Living with parents that always argue and fight in front of you is something I never wish for my children. Mainly alcohol-fuelled, it was a toxic environment. It got to a point when my grandparents, who lived in Cornwall, one day turned up with a van and packed some of our belongings into it, and we left Birmingham for good. We moved to Cornwall without my Dad and made a new life for ourselves. I was too relieved in my eleven-year-old mind to tell anyone that a family member had also been grooming me. I chose to block it out. The wrongness of this choice wouldn't become obvious for many years.

They were the best years. They were spending most days on the beach. My grandparents were a huge part of my life, and I will be forever grateful for the opportunity they opened up to me.

Home life was great, but school life turned out to be not so great. Trying to fit into a school where I had already missed the first year when everyone bonds and makes friendship groups was difficult. I was the new girl. Boys showed interest, but the girls were wary of me and I found myself flitting between groups hoping to mingle in some- how. I stood out with my 'Brummy' accent. Girls were curious or just instantly didn't like me.

I said something flippant one day to another girl about something that was nothing but it caused a reaction and from then on, my life was made hell at school. It was a pivotal moment for my school life to become a daily attack.

A group formed within my age group and I got taunted daily. Spat at, ink flicked on the back of my shirts, pushed, shoved and laughed at. The worst was that nobody wanted to be my friend. Who wanted to get attacked for being my friend?

One day I got followed by 'the gang' to a local tuck shop where I was so frightened I ran into the phone box. I picked up the phone but had no money, and they were banging on it so heavily the glass cracked. I feared for my life as they just egged each other on to do worse to me every single time.

I also realise now that this was when I became strong mentally. People can do things physically to you, but as long as you have the mental capacity to stay strong and rise above it, you will get through. This is how I got through my school years. It was crap, but I did it, and I did it with integrity. I never reacted, I just let them get on with it and knew life would be better after school.

Bullying is not something I would wish on anyone as it can feel so isolating and equally terrifying. That feeling of being alone and scared is not a good place to be. If, however, you are going through something similar please take comfort in the fact you are never alone. The biggest advocate you have is yourself. You will become stronger from this and you find out new things about yourself which will help you throughout the rest of your life. Yes, it hurts, but go away, lick those wounds and remember wounds always heal. The skin becomes thicker and tougher and so will you!

I went to college and did well but realised there was a big world out there for me to explore. So to my Mum's utter horror, I signed up to the Army and left two months shy of my nineteenth birthday. I joined the Army medical core and wanted to work up the ranks and help others this way instead.

I thoroughly enjoyed Army life. It wasn't easy, especially in basic training. I watched others drop like flies throughout the twelve-week process, and I became determined not to be a drop out too. No matter what it took, I was going to be in the passing out parade and complete all the timed runs and exercises. Being one of the slowest runners to begin with, it was a challenge, but I did it. I was so proud of myself. My determination and grit to succeed, not for anyone else but myself, was so great that it fuelled and pushed me on through the blisters and all.

The Army teaches you so much. The main thing I took from it is that I can achieve anything if I put my mind to it. It does not matter what other people put you through, it's having the mental capacity to stay strong. This is what gets you through...the sense of belonging. You're such a tight-knit group of individuals with the same values and strengths. You do feel unstoppable. I suggest everyone having a group of likeminded individuals to be there for you, listen, learn and watch out for you and push you at all times.

I moved on through the Army up the ranks, becoming a medic and then more specifically moving into the operating theatre and training to become an ODP (Operating Department Practitioner). I specialised in; Trauma and Orthopaedics, Vascular and Plastic Surgery.

I had the best times, and it was an absolute pleasure. It was fun and exhilarating, working and living with my best friends, living my best life, travelling and working. Although you do see things that can't be unseen, you get through it as a unit. The camaraderie was key.

After a few years, the tight-knit group I had become accustomed to slowly split up as we moved our career paths in different directions. It wasn't the same anymore.

I decided to leave the Army and go back home and get a job at Truro hospital to finish off my training. I have to say I missed the Army, but my confidence and attitude to life were incredible. I knew who I was, where I was going, and nobody could stop me. Life was just wonderful.

I then decided to go travelling with my best friend out of the blue. I am always out for adventure, and I had itchy feet being back home so we flew to South Africa.

Oh, how I fell in love with this place. After just splitting with a cheating boyfriend it was the best medicine for me. Soon into our trip, we met two boys on a bus. I wasn't particularly interested in boys, with the recent breakup, but my friend was always interested in any good looking guys.

Everywhere we went, these two boys were. My friend got with Nick, and they spent a lot of time together, which meant I was left with the other one. The Joys! We did get on well, though, and as a group of four had the best times. From South Africa, we went to Thailand and then Vicki and I were going to be in Bali for Christmas and New Year. The boys stayed in Thailand, and we would then meet them in Australia in the New Year.

We left the day before Christmas Eve and asked them if they wanted to come with us to Bali. They politely declined so on we went. On Christmas Eve, we received an email to say they had changed their minds and were on their way to stay with us. We met up with them, had a fantastic Christmas Day together but it was also very bizarre: I'm a traditional Christmas Day girl at heart.

On Boxing Day we got up, and something wasn't quite right outside. It felt eerie. We turned the TV on, and the news was talking about a tsunami that had hit Thailand. We were so shocked and sad.

My first thought was to fly to Thailand to help in the recovery and use my medical skills in any way I could, but I couldn't get there.

We came to realise later that the hotel the boys were staying in got washed away, and at that moment two things happened. Firstly, the sadness knowing that we had probably lost friends who would still have been there, but also that if the boys had not come to Bali, they wouldn't be here. It was such a shock to us. One of those moments that take your breath away as if you have been sucker-punched.

The boys hadn't told their families they had followed two young blondes to Bali. The phone lines were all down where we were so it was by email they could let them know they were still alive. From that day we did every-thing together. I realised I also really liked this guy, Dan. His family were so happy he had met me because if he hadn't, he wouldn't be here with us. Dan, to this day, calls me his guardian angel. He calls me a lot of other things too. Some bad but mostly good!

When we eventually flew home after nine months of trav-elling around the world, I was at another crossroads. I lived in Cornwall; Dan lived in Dorset. Being a realist, I said goodbye to Dan at Heathrow. Told him it had been amazing, but long-distance relationships weren't my thing.

The very next day my Mum came running into my bedroom to tell me there was a guy at the door. I walked out, and there was Dan with a massive bunch of flowers telling me he missed me and couldn't live without me! Me being my honest self as always, stated that it hadn't been 24 hours, and if he was going to buy me flowers again, please don't buy Lilies as I don't like them. I know I know, what the hell, Hayley?

Not long after this, Dan found us a house in Dorset. I got a job in a private hospital just outside of Salisbury, and so I moved to be with him. We were really happy. We had a few ups and downs and big bumps, but on the whole, we were happy.

We had D'Arcy in 2007 and thirteen months later, her brother Harrison was born. I know you do the maths, it's ridiculous! This birth wasn't as straightforward, however, and Dan nearly lost Harrison and me. But thanks to the team I worked with at the hospital, they saved us. A very harrowing experience though.

But we got through it, and life carried on relatively normally. I was enjoying maternity leave, but looking forward to going back to work. Work was where I came alive and what I had worked so hard to achieve.

THE DAY MY WORLD CHANGED.

The day before I was due back to work, I decided to go out for a drive with the children. Just a chilled drive.

On the way home, I was involved in a car accident. A van went into the back of me and shunted me into the stationary car in front. Luckily the children were ok. They were screaming, and I knew even though they had just been through horrific trauma, they were alive. I, on the other hand, went in and out of consciousness. The fire service turned up to cut the roof off my car, and there were police and paramedics.

Two things happened this day: one, my physical injuries and two, my mental injuries.

The accident triggered off something my eleven-year-old self had locked away in the deepest depths of my mind. The grooming.

I went into full panic mode wanting to see where D'Arcy was, who she was with and I had it in my head that she was not safe with any man, suddenly. It was harrowing. Nobody could understand me or help. I was being told to stay still as I may have spinal injuries, but I wanted to see my children.

I was sent to the hospital where I was given my long list of injuries but also this sense of panic for my daughter was just too much to take.

Now, I am a woman who believes that as long as you have the cognitive ability and keep your mind strong and healthy, positive and determined, you can get through anything.

Unfortunately, this had taken away my mental capacity, and it had awakened nightmares from my seven-to-eleven-year-old self which I was now projecting onto my daughter.

I didn't want D'Arcy out of my sight, not even with Dan. It was utterly crippling because I wasn't physically able to look after her. I had to go to London for an inpatient stay at the Wellington hospital. Rehabilitation was hard. I was on so many different drugs to help with the nerve damage in my arm and hand, the back pain from the spinal fracture, the neck pain and migraines while still frantically dealing with this childhood trauma, it was all too much for me.

I broke down. I turned into a zombie and half the woman I was. It broke me, and the shame and guilt of this from my strong independent self was heartbreaking.

When I got home, I had constant reviews, check-ups, and home reviews to see what could be adapted for me, and continually being told 'life-changing' trauma was sad. Every time I was told something new, I lost another piece of myself. The day I finally got told I could no longer work in my chosen career as I was uninsurable with my disabilities, was the day the last piece of me was taken. I went home and became that zombie. I didn't know who I was anymore. A shell of my former self that had constant pain and also fear for my daughter being left with another man. I didn't know why. That's how deep and dark I had hidden the past events in my brain. I was ashamed to tell anyone and so confused by it all.

I look back on this time and realise just how lucky I am to have found Dan. He is my guardian angel.

But, when I found myself lying on the bed screaming into the pillow, a flicker of the old Hayley came back through at that moment. I saw what I still had and what I still could do. I also realised life is always throwing curveballs at us; it's how we pick that ball up and throw it right back that counts. We get to choose our path. We get to choose the light instead of the dark. Everything that happens in life to us we can't change or undo, but we can choose how we deal with it.At every step in your life you get to choose how you deal with pain, loss and curve balls. It's the ability in each and every one of us to choose to make that change and make it a positive one. Life is for living. So choose to live your best life always. No matter what your circumstances.

RISING UP

I decided to choose positivity and light and get the old me back.

It was hard work. Firstly, I checked myself into counselling to deal with that disgusting trauma that was affecting me so much. With this still in my head, I couldn't get through anything else.

The most traumatic experience was going back through what happened to me. Also for me to get through it, I had to tell family members. My Mum, my grandparents, my Dad and my sisters. What my sisters didn't realise is, I was always protecting them from harm by doing as I was told to keep them safe. My intentions were always to keep them from harm. My parents were dealing with their own demons at the time this was happening so I couldn't rely on them. It was hard to tell them and also challenging to deal with how some of them just shook it off, if I am honest. But it wasn't my awful secret anymore. I held no shame or blame for what happened to me. What I did realise is my caring spirit was always there inside of me. The protector.

After dealing with the mental trauma, the physical trauma was next. I worked hard to ween off the drugs. They did not help me; they were a placebo effect that stunted my mental growth. I got back to doing exercise slowly. Because the payout was big, the insurance company wanted to 'catch me out'. This was another thing to deal with along the way. It was hard because no amount of money would give me what I really wanted: this to have never happened to me.

Once I got back to some kind of normality where I could get dressed, look after the children, live with the pain and discomfort, I started to think about what was next.

I could no longer work in the medical profession, but there must be something else out there for me. I could not sit or stand for very long periods, so this kind of stopped me from working for someone else. I needed flexibility.

Within my rehab, I wanted to use my hand again which I had lost use of due to the nerve damage. I was using a stress ball to help with dexterity and strength. One day this turned to icing. I used to sit with my Nan every Saturday and decorate cakes. So I started to do the same to help with my rehab and have something to do. This then turned to baking, and within months I was regularly baking. Dan decided to start selling my bakes at a local farmers' market for me, and it was a huge success. I then got asked to make a birthday cake, and then this led to weddings. In 2012, with positivity, determination and Dan by my side, my cake business was born.

It took off quickly, and within twelve months, I was fully booked every week and creating to my heart's content. I built the business up from nothing. A little spark of imagination and not letting anything stop me. I was back.

BUT SO WERE THE BULLIES

My business grew every year, doubling in orders and income. It was incredible, and I feel like baking saved me. It gave me a passion mixed with my stubborn determination always to succeed. I felt like nothing could throw me off track again. How wrong could I be?

The online space was growing and I realised it was the perfect place to be seen by more clients and grow without investing too much if anything at all. What I didn't realise is the cake space online can be so very bitchy and cruel. When one person takes an instant dislike to what you are doing, and they have a small following of like-minded people, it can be easy for them to bully behind a screen with their keyboard. A post on my Facebook page one day was used to fuel this dislike towards me, and within an hour, I had fifty or so comments from others with nasty, bitchy things to say. All over a Christmas wedding cake, I had made. They didn't believe I had made the chocolate balls, which looked like Christmas baubles. I kid you not! Seriously, this is what they chose to invest their time and efforts in from one person goading them who didn't like the fact that I was successful. It wasn't me she didn't like – how could she, she didn't know me, and neither did this group of idiots. But jealousy has a nasty way of rearing its ugly head, and it got so upsetting. I was so terrified my clients would be reading this stuff that I took my Facebook page down.

It felt like I was back at school again but worse. Online trolling and bullying is so damaging. I had just come through hell and got myself back together, and here I was again faced with another traumatic experience to deal with. At first, I didn't feel strong enough to stick around and be constantly abused by this group. It really damaged my confidence and my happiness. I decided I would start again in another field; Interior design. I did an online course and thought I could use my creative side in interiors. I loved the course and gained confidence but partway through the course, I couldn't believe I was going to give up something that had saved me. Made me whole again. Why let the bully win!

So, while finishing my interior design course, I invested in my branding and marketing and launched myself as a high-end luxury cake designer. Aiming higher and destined for bigger and better things. It worked. My business has been so successful to this day. I've honed my skills and carved a way for me to be recognised in my field. I have even travelled abroad to deliver cakes for high profile clients. My flower craft has even taken me into interior design with a high profile interior designer, and I'm now making works of art, literally in cake and porcelain. I look back on this time now and realise that starting and completing the interior design course had set me on a path for even bigger success, fuelled with determination to grow bigger and better than the bullies!

RISING UP AND STAYING STRONG

The future is bright for me, and I have now invested in a cake academy where I am helping other cake businesses grow and become successful. Helping others is what I have always had within me, from an early age with my sisters, through to the Army and my medical career, and now to cake designers, at the same time, creating beautiful works of art and becoming an entrepreneur in my own right on my own path.

Yes, I have had trips and stumbles throughout my life, but I am made of strong stuff. Shit happens to every one of us throughout our lives. Nobody is exempt from hurt or pain.

Some have it more than others, but every one of us will go through it at some point in our lives. We can't change what happens to us. It's how we mentally deal with it that counts. Use it as fuel to become a better you. Look at everything you have around you. Life is beautiful. You are beautiful, and you can rise up and push through if you stay strong and positive. Always remember with dark there is light. With a stop, there is a start. With a no, there is a yes. The pattern is there, positive and negative. You get to choose how to look at an event in your life and how you deal with it.

I am a testament to this. I choose to rise up and be strong, choosing to not let anyone tell me I can't do something or make me feel I am inferior. I decide what I want to do and I go for it. Always with grace and kindness to all.

Don't let events, trauma or people in your past frame your future. You get to choose where you are destined to be. Surround yourself with positivity and kindness and fuel in your belly, and you will be unstoppable!

ABOUT THE AUTHOR

Hayley Jones

Hayley Jones is the founder of the luxury wedding cake studio Hayley Elizabeth Cake Design, working with high profile clients alongside prestigious venues and suppliers all over the UK. She also educates, inspires and supports other cake business owners in learning sugarcraft and cake skills through her online school, Hayley Elizabeth Cake Academy.

Hayley is a former member of the armed forces with a medical background, specialising in the surgical field of Trauma and Orthopaedics, Vascular and Plastic surgery. She has drawn upon these skills as the foundations of her business and personal growth. Together with personal trauma, this background has shaped her into a woman who knows how to achieve success with integrity and grace - and is now helping others achieve the same.

She has won many awards and accolades and has been featured in numerous publications including magazines, blogs and television shows, such as Brides, Elle and Love My Dress and National T.V. With an established presence in the wedding industry, she is now carving her way in the interior design world with one-off pieces of art, utilising her sugarcraft knowledge and skill in conjunction with her passion for home decor.

When Hayley is not working you will find her with her family Dan, D'Arcy, Harrison and Dexter the beagle in the New Forest or at the beach. Exercise has kept Hayley mentally achieving throughout her life and it is something she continues to do fondly with Dexter, allowing her to continue in her mission to bring beauty to life, and help others create the businesses and lives of their dreams.

CONTACT:

EMAIL:
hello@hayleyelizabethcakedesign.com

WEBSITES:
www.hayleyelizabethcakedesign.com
www.hayleyelizabethcakeacademy.com

INSTAGRAM:
www.instagram.com/hayleyelizabethcakeacademy

FACEBOOK: group for cake designers
www.facebook.com/groups/HayleyElizabeththetoptier

FACEBOOK: page for cake academy
www.facebook.com/hayleyelizabethcakeacademy

PINTEREST:
www.pinterest.com/hayleyelizabethcakeacademy

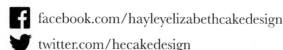

facebook.com/hayleyelizabethcakedesign
twitter.com/hecakedesign
instagram.com/hayleyelizabethcakedesign
pinterest.com/hayleyelizabethcakedesign
linkedin.com/in/hayley-jones

9

JACQUIE LAWES

When I grow up, I want to be... me

We've all been asked at one point or another what we want to be when we grow up. What does 'grow up' even mean? When does that happen? I've always been someone that loves to have a joke and am a bit of a big kid really. Have I grown up? Am I still growing up? Or was that simply a generic 'when you're an adult' stage? Who knows.

I recently asked my nearly five-year-old daughter what she wanted to be when she was older. I'd assumed she would say something most children say, like a doctor, a vet, an actor, a musician, a princess, etc. But no, her response was absolutely perfect. Without thinking about it she responded with, "When I grow up, Mummy, I want to be me."

That's when it hit me. Who am I? What makes me, well, me? I am 'Mummy' but I am so much more than that – but I guess I kind of just forgot to be just me too.

Ever since I can remember I have had two passions in life. Animals and art. When those around me had dreams of being a doctor, an actor, a teacher and all the other things they encourage you to be at school, I was dreaming about being either a zookeeper or a photographer (hell, the two combined would be amazing!). I never really thought much about what I wanted to be when I grew up, more what I wanted to do or the type of thing I would do. I loved school but I excelled when I was able to be creative or take part in some kind of fun activity rather than reading a book, writing an essay or listening to a lecture.

I found it really difficult to absorb information through reading or listening to a teacher who didn't have a fun and energetic approach to teaching. Exams were my absolute nightmare! Whilst my peers and even my brothers would study and take in all the information (and keep it lodged somewhere in their brain ready to unlock when the appropriate question came up), I would forget absolutely everything the second I turned the exam paper. Literally everything.

I'd study for hours/days/sometimes weeks with reading, listening to lessons, writing notes, highlighting pretty much my whole textbook. It would go in but instantly fall straight back out again. If it wasn't something that interested me it just wouldn't ever sink in. I tried every method I could but in exams I would just about scrape by, whereas in coursework I would absolutely smash it!

Completing coursework meant I was able to complete the work in my own time and in my own way, working in a way that I was happy and confident in. Being in a room full of students in silence, the sound of the clock ticking, the pacing of the teacher who would be watching out for any cheating or communicating between pupils, seeing the 'brainy' classmates turn their pages before I'd even finished working out what the first question was asking. It was just an uncomfortable, stressful environment and not once did I ever get the feeling I'd done well having left the room. I would hear others bouncing out of the exam room saying, "That was so much easier than I thought it would be," when I'd be sweating about my poor attempt to answer half the questions in the entire paper. It just wasn't fun and fun was something I wanted for my working career ahead.

Let me ask you something for a minute. How much fun do you have doing what you do? Are you working doing something that makes you genuinely happy? Something that you're so passionate about, it doesn't even feel like work at all because you absolutely love what you do. Or are you working in a job you don't really enjoy because you feel it's just what's done. You get up, go to work so you can pay the bills, come home and do it all over again the next day.

Many people very close to me have worked in careers they don't enjoy. Working overtime for that extra bonus in the monthly wages. Being taken for granted in a job they don't even like but just going along with it, perhaps for several years (or even decades!) because it's what's done. Sound familiar?

But why shouldn't you feel like you're having fun in what you do? Whatever fun is to you, you can 100% have a career doing what you love.

I always wanted to fit in when I was growing up. To be liked and to make people laugh. Being cheeky and loud by nature this ended up with me always being caught out if I was misbehaving at school. Many classes would include 'Jacquie, are you listening?' or 'Jacquie, can you share the joke with the rest of the class?' from the teacher, often resulting in me being sent out the classroom for 'being disruptive'.

Don't get me wrong, I wasn't naughty at school. I worked bloody hard and I always loved school. Sure there were lessons I absolutely hated and could never find the energy or enthusiasm to take in what was being said, but I knew I wasn't going to need Chemistry, Physics, Religious Studies or even History for the career path I was hoping to take so it often seemed a waste of time taking part in those lessons, to me.

I would get into trouble because I loved the attention I would get from my peers when I'd do stupid things. Being the joker. The class clown.

My school reports would always say 'works hard and is enthusiastic but could do with a little less talking in class' or 'she has the potential to do amazingly but needs to focus in class'.

When I turned sixteen I couldn't wait to get a job. I just wanted to have some independence and earn some money. So I did what most school kids did and got a paper round (which I absolutely HATED). The only plus side was I got to see some cute dogs doing my round but that was it. So that didn't last long and I ended up getting a job working at a kennels which even now was one of my favourite jobs of all.

Spending the whole day at the weekend cleaning out, playing with and feeding the dogs was an absolute dream job for me. I have always been obsessed with dogs so to get paid to look after them was just amazing. I was doing what I was so passionate about.

It made me realise... doing all these lessons at school so I could eventually apply to uni and follow the standard procedure of the education path, it just wasn't me. It wasn't what I wanted to do.

I loved school but I knew I wanted to do something I loved, and get there without having to go to uni or college. I just wanted to get started on my career without having to spend another few years studying.

I thought long and hard about what I wanted to do and as much as I would have loved a career with animals, my true passion that is just in me was to be creative. I loved studying art, photography and fashion textiles as A Levels at school and I knew I wanted to pursue a career where I could be creative.

So it came to the point when you have to start filling in your university applications at school. I knew I didn't want to do it but being the only student in my year group who didn't want to apply to uni, I was told by my teachers that I would need to apply because 'if you want to work in media or the creative industry you need to study at uni otherwise you're going to struggle to get a job when you apply'.

If anyone tells me I can't do something or advises me not to do something, I'm sure as hell going to do it to prove them wrong! It only makes me more determined. So I ignored the teachers. I was the only one in my year at school who didn't apply to uni but I still worked my arse off at school because I loved my subjects and I really wanted to do well in my A Levels.

When summer came and all my friends were heading off to uni or starting their gap year adventures, I applied for a job working in Visual Merchandising and you know what, I bloody got it. I got to do what I loved, being creative and getting paid for it!

It opened up the doors to me being able to work in the creative industry. Designing and setting up window displays, decorating the store for each seasonal event (which was particularly exciting for me at Christmas, being a complete festive nut). The one thing I didn't enjoy was the pay. It wasn't great but it got me on the ladder and I enjoyed the job so I was happy to stay there, although I knew I wanted something more and to be earning more.

I decided to sign up to a recruitment agency to see what other creative jobs were out there. I went in, had my interview and told them what I was looking for. My absolute dream at the time was to work in a photography studio. I didn't really care what I did, I was happy to be an assistant, a runner, whatever came up. Living outside of London, where most of the good creative roles were, I knew I was asking for a lot. The agency even told me jobs like this very rarely come up and when they do they want someone with experience in a studio.

So I knew even after my interview at the agency that my chances were slim.

But fate was on my side. The agency had contacted a few photography studios in the area and when I received a phone call (that same day!) to tell me one studio specialising in advertising photography was looking for a Studio Manager as their current one was just about to leave following her four weeks' notice and by chance they hadn't advertised the role anywhere. I was invited to an interview the following day.

I couldn't believe it. This was my chance to get a job doing exactly what I dreamed of doing. I didn't have long to prep and get myself ready for my interview but I got my photography portfolio together to show my work (I wasn't even sure if that was relevant since it wasn't for a job as a photographer but it showed I had a keen interest in photography). I had some examples of the work I'd done in my current role and nervously drove to the studio for my interview.

I gave myself a good talking to, told myself to just be me and show how I'm the best person for this role.

When I went in, they had a huge roomset set up in one studio and some models were in the other for some toys or something. It was really dark apart from the studio lights and I was shown around by one of the team before I was introduced to the manager who was interviewing me. It was literally the most laid-back interview ever. He looked at my portfolio, asked me a few questions about my interests, what I'd done to date and was I into photography, etc. Then he followed (around ten minutes later) with, great, when can you start?

I wasn't sure if he was joking or not, but being a bit of a joker I responded with, "Um, is now too soon?"

So if you're following the typical academic path that you're told the whole way through the early stage of your life, this is proof that just because it's the 'norm', if it doesn't feel like it's the route you want to take yourself, that's ok! Sometimes it's ok to take a risk and go against what you're being told to do because only you know what you want to achieve in life and how you want to do it.

I worked there for over six years and loved it. Even now it was probably my favourite job because no two days were the same. I was responsible for the whole studio and all productions as I was the main point of contact for all of our clients. It was such an amazing opportunity to work there and opened up lots of doors for me in my creative career.

My career then followed with me continuing with my passions in the creative industry, from photography and video content for a leading retailer to working in a graphic and web design team specialising in brand design, packaging and video production.

I loved my jobs and have been so fortunate to only ever work in creative roles that have helped me to progress in a career that I was passionate about. I was doing what I wanted to do, what made me, me!

When I had my first daughter, that's when everything changed. Like many women, I wasn't able to return to the job I loved because I simply had a choice of going back full time and not seeing my daughter, or leaving completely. So that's what I did.

It was a scary time, losing a salary in our household. But we managed. It was a few months later that I realised, I wasn't being me. I was mum, all the time. Don't get me wrong, I absolutely love being a mum; my kids are my whole world but I also know that unless I'm being me and doing what I love, I am never truly happy.

So I made the decision to start my own business. I wanted to be creative. To design something but I didn't know what.

Having designed some wedding stationery for some friends during my maternity leave, I thought to myself, 'I could do that! I could set up a wedding stationery business!' and me being me, I jumped straight in. Within a couple of months I had a website, had some orders coming in and I was actually running my own business and people were buying from me. It was amazing!

In the first year of running my business I won the award for Best Wedding Stationery for the region in the UK's biggest wedding awards and continued to win the following two years, which was just amazing. But as time went on, I realised I was producing the same kind of thing over and over and, yes, I was making a difference to my clients and giving them their beautiful wedding stationery that they loved, but I wanted more. I wanted to make a bigger impact on people's lives. I branched out into brand design and photography, which is what I'd spent most of my working career doing so I have no idea why I didn't think to start with this rather than the wedding stationery, but hey!

I massively uplevelled my business, invested a lot in getting it right and also worked on my own mindset and confidence. Because even though I've always been the cheeky one who was a bit noisy in school, I'm not a confident person. I'm an introvert and like to fit in with the crowd. But to get noticed and stand out from my competitors I knew I had to sort myself out, put on my big girl pants and give myself that boost to have the confidence to show up and get myself and my business visible.

How could I bring my own personality into what I was doing, though, when I wasn't even sure who I really was? Sure, I was a mum, a wife, an entrepreneur, but when I wasn't doing any of those things, what was I doing? I'd got so wrapped up in looking after the kids, sorting the house out (trying to at least, anyway!), making sure I had time for my hubby and I to have some time together. But when was my time? When was I allowing myself to just be me?

It's true: when you become a mum everything changes, and with the challenges of running a business (or two in my case) it feels near impossible to find time for anything other than feeding, entertaining, going to dance classes, school runs, tidying up after the kids, only for them to just make just as much mess again in about five seconds. It can easily feel like you're on a conveyor belt. Get up, sort the kids out, eat breakfast, school run, entertain our youngest, sort lunch, try to have a couple of client calls or respond to some emails, snacks, school run, post school meltdown to manage, dinner, bedtime routine. Once they're in bed I then get to start work for the day.

I'm forever getting told, 'Wow, you're smashing it,' or asked, 'How do you do it all with two young children?' and the truth is, most of the time I don't feel like I've got my shit together at all. I feel like a blue arsed fly rushing around like crazy, dotting from one thing to another. BUT determination, passion and love for what I do, and the goals I have on my dream board (which naturally includes holidays, a bigger home, new car, space for more dogs etc.), give me focus to keep going and I'm so excited to see where my business goes.

I've spent a lot of time blocking out my diary, scheduling and automating my workflows to allow enough time to be Mum, run my businesses, be a wife and allow time for me to do the things that I love. I've completely transformed my business since I launched. I started out as a hobbyist and now I'm a multi award winning entrepreneur running an agency with my own team of freelancers.

Why did I decide to choose this path in my career? That's easy. Because not only was I able to do what I loved but I was able to make a difference to others too. I see so many women creating or selling amazing products and who have huge amounts of talent, yet they undercharge and undersell themselves and what they do. They don't feel good enough to charge their worth and they lack confidence in what they do.

When I get to work with these women and help them to create a brand for their business it's so rewarding for me as a designer, and for me to see the difference in not only their business but their confidence and mindset. They finally start to see themselves as entrepreneurs and feel like they can finally charge their worth. That for me is just incredible and it's the main reason why I specialise in branding for product-based businesses.

It also means I'm able to bring all of my skills and experiences from over fifteen years in the creative industry to transform their branding and, in turn, their brand to take their business to the next level. I absolutely love what I do and I'm so grateful to have had the opportunities I've had over the years and the support from my family and friends. I'm able to be me, 100% me, in my life and business. My clients book with me because they want to work with me, not anyone else, not another designer or photographer, but me. I don't have to hide behind my branding; I'm not confined to having to work in a certain way or when my rota says I have to. I can just be me and work the way I want to, which allows me to have the work/life balance I want.

Sure, I could have stuck with the easy option of continuing to be a full-time mum and not working at all. I could have even continued with my well-established wedding stationery business, but this wasn't allowing me to be the real me. It didn't ignite that fire inside me.

My goals in life are to be happy. Not rich. Not famous. Not even successful, really. To be happy and for my family to be happy too. That probably sounds really cheesy, but it's absolutely true!

The most important thing I've learned in life is to always just be me. To love who I am and surround myself with people who love me too. You can never please everyone and not everyone will like you, and that's a good thing. How boring would it be if everyone liked you?

I'm just being me and hopefully my daughters will grow up to be 100% them too.

So when I continue to grow up I want to be me!

ABOUT THE AUTHOR

Jacquie Lawes

Jacquie Lawes is a branding expert and designer with over fifteen years expertise in product branding, from visual merchandising and creative content production, to branding identity and packaging design.

Design and creative content production is all Jacquie has ever known in her working career. It's what she is most passionate about and Jacquie loves nothing more than to be creative herself and teach others how to create a luxury branded experience for their business.

Jacquie set up a luxury wedding stationery design business in 2016 after having her first daughter and being unable to return to the job she loved.

Multiple award wins later, Jacquie now works with other creative female entrepreneurs to create a luxury brand experience for their customers.

Jacquie's mission is to transform as many women as possible from seeing themselves as a hobbyist into an entrepreneur with a confident brand.

CONTACT:

WEBSITE
www.baileyandroo.com

instagram.com/baileyandroo

10

KATE MORRIS-BATES

The 3 C's of Life - Chances, Choices and Changes

INTRODUCTION

"You're braver than you believe, and stronger than you seem, and smarter than you think."

— CHRISTOPHER ROBIN (A. A. MILNE)

Somewhere between my high heeled exit from corporate life in my mid-thirties, and the flat pumped entrance to being a mum in my forties I lost myself.

That strong, confident, independent woman disappeared. Not sure when and not sure where, but I woke up one day and, oooooffff, there it was - the right-between-the-eyes realisation that she was not there anymore. Or at least she was not somewhere I could reach or see her.

It had not happened overnight. Hands up, it was a gradual process of life changing circumstances and choices, along with the words and behaviours of others and not having a crystal ball which could enable me to see what the future held and navigate some pretty difficult times.

What did happen overnight, though, was the realisation that if I wanted to change my life the only person who was going to make this happen was me. I had a choice – to take a chance and change the status quo.

I chose to find that woman again through a messy, challenging, topsy-turvy kaleidoscope of self-help books, coaching, qualifications, new business ventures, training courses and tribe finding. Spending shed loads of money and time on reconnecting with my power. Some things were worth it. Others not at all. I discovered people who enriched my life. I left people behind who dragged me down. I made these choices and I stand by them, whether they worked out as I thought I wanted, or whether they did not.

By sharing my story and my learnings, it is my intention to help you understand that it is totally within your gift to step into your power, to own who you are, to accept your past, to have courage and ultimately to reconnect with your inner Goddess. And by Goddess I do not mean Goddess in a schmaltzy-flowers-in-your-hair way. I mean in a strong, awesome, confident, healthy woman who is totally owning herself kind of way. Because you DO have this choice, whoever you are.

There are three Cs of Life: Chances, Choices and Changes. You must take a chance to make a choice and change your life if you are to rise and give yourself the opportunity to be the person YOU want to be.

ROLL BACK

"I can't go back to yesterday because I was a different person then."

— ALICE IN WONDERLAND (LEWIS CARROLL)

I was not always a Pain & Skin Specialist, Acupuncturist, Chinese Medicine Practitioner, Coach, Clinic Director, and unashamed female empowerment soapbox owner.

Nope. For over twenty years I was six-figure earning corporate hard hitter. A high heeled woman in a grey suited man's world. I loved it. By the time I was 34 I was a Top 100 Exec leader in a huge national company, leading 600+ people and being responsible for hundreds of millions of pounds. It was one of the biggest jobs of its kind in the UK. I enjoyed the finer things life had to offer to a strong single woman in her early 30s. I stood up for myself and what I believed in, but I was always kind, acting with integrity. I valued myself. And it was paying off. It is also when I met my husband too.

That is the point when life changed, without me choosing it.

ROCK BOTTOM IS A FOUNDATION STONE

"Rock bottom became the solid foundation on which I rebuilt my life."

— J.K. ROWLING

When you lose one baby through miscarriage, your perspective changes. When you lose six, your life changes. When it happens inside two years, your world changes.

I had not wanted children until I met my now husband in my thirties. It wasn't in my life plan. Being a female is not a synonym for being mum in my view. We have no right to assume we know or understand another woman's choices, situation, feelings, or experiences on this matter, but we do have a responsibility to respect them. I truly believe that had I not met my husband I would have happily continued living my childless life to the full, but I know this is not the same for everyone and I honour another woman's feelings in this space.

However, it had not occurred to me that if I had wanted children that it would be anything other than straightforward. In my naivety I thought having a baby was going to be easy. Everyone else, or at least so it seemed, got pregnant easily enough. And stayed pregnant until a healthy baby entered the world. I had heard about IVF; I had heard about miscarriages, but I understood nothing about them. Nobody I knew really talked about it, and I had no reason to learn about it: blissful ignorance.

When my husband and I met we both had successful careers, had had a "life" before each other and were loving our thirties – a time of abundance. We started trying for a baby soon after we married, when I was 36 years old, and within six months there was a little blue line on the pregnancy test.

Not for long though. Eight weeks into my pregnancy I experienced my first loss. Nothing had prepared me or my husband for it. Not just the physical effects, but the searing grief, the loneliness, the fear, the lack of explanation and the confusion. Not to mention the lack of control over my own body. But I recovered, read up and I was reassured that whilst it happened to one in four women, the chances of it happening again were low, despite my age and being in apparent good health.

I went on to conceive five more times and lost all five at differing stages of pregnancy. I was told every time I went to the GP that there was nothing "wrong" with me or my husband and it was all down to bad luck. I almost got past the first trimester with my second pregnancy, but this ended during the night of New Year's Eve whilst in our campervan. We were staying at a remote campsite with no phone signal at the foot of England's highest mountain.

Driving two hundred miles home on January 1st to go to hospital, knowing that another baby was lost, was one of the darkest days of my life. I have experienced challenging times prior to this but this was THE single most memorable day in my entire life, when I literally felt I had zero power and therefore zero choice over what was happening to me. I felt like I was wearing a strait jacket whilst caged in my own body and my own head.

I hit rock bottom that day, and in the months afterwards. I am not going to pretend otherwise. But this single event more than any other taught me that nothing is permanent; the storm did pass eventually, and I got through it, albeit no longer in a state of blissful ignorance.

Four miscarriages down, I also got to the point where I decided to stand up for myself and my husband. I was no longer prepared to accept the wishy-washy dumbed down explanations by non-experts who were not invested in our future. I chose to question and challenge the medical system and make it clear my husband and I deserved the help of specialist fertility experts. I wanted to understand for myself if our situation was due to something other than "bad luck".

This was done with my eyes wide open that I might not like the outcome to my questions or get the result I wanted. But I made the choice to pursue it.

Making a conscious choice gave me my power back. Things started changing from that moment. I had my rainbow baby.

PLAYING THE VICTIM IS EASY

"You are a victim of the rules you live by."

— JENNY HOLZER

Work was also an epic shitshow at this exact time. Disastrous financial results plus a series of mismanagement crises resulted in new faces at the most senior tables. New faces who wanted to bring in their own people to make the changes required. With my big girl pants on I know that is what happens, but it is what it is - nothing short of a professional hatchet job. An example of something in "professional life" that can make you feel your knees are being kicked from behind whilst you wear a blindfold. The feeling of paranoia can take over your every waking moment if you let it - and do not recognise it for what it is… business culture and business behaviour. It might not be right, but in most cases it is not personal.

However, it is tough to be wise when you are getting a metaphorical shoeing every day, and easier and simpler to slot yourself into the role of victim whilst the bullies dine out at your expense. I know the word "Victim" can be very triggering and I want to say I am not talking about victims of abuse of any kind; I am talking about a victim mentality, which is when you believe it is always someone else's fault for bad things happening to you. The victim mentality blames others for their circumstances – when something happens, they do not take responsibility for their actions.

Having a victim mentality means you are waiting for someone to rescue you, rather than focusing on your options to save yourself. That might be a zinger of a message for some, and it hit me like a sharp stick between the eyes when I realised it too. I chose to put myself in that victim box because I didn't get off the hamster wheel long enough to think about it differently, and I didn't invite anyone to help me think differently either. Ouch.

Years of underinvestment, severe cost cutting, a merry-go-round of business strategies and an intra-company political circus made life hard; very frickin' hard. I excelled at my job, but I was not a maker of magic. You cannot make a silk purse from a sow's ear no matter how hard you try. It took its toll on me – I worked 80+ hour weeks, commuted hours every day and ate on the hoof, whilst trying to have a healthy pregnancy. That was not entirely work's "fault". It was partly mine. Yeah, they didn't exactly make it easy for me but with the benefit of 20/20 vision in hindsight, I can see I was making the choice to prioritise work over my health, I just didn't see it that way at the time. I felt I didn't have a choice, which was not the case. I just didn't want to think about my choices, as it would mean changing something which could threaten my income and my ego. Serious ouch.

I played along with the unspoken narrative of "sucking it up", which was wrong. I could have chosen to be brave and say no to the ridiculous demands. Or I could have chosen to walk away sooner. Or I could have asked for help. I did have those choices, but I was so "in" the thick of it I just didn't see them. And this is what happens when we are in the middle of a situation: we struggle to rise above the melee and think clearly.

The work challenges magnified as the number of lost pregnancies increased, and my health deteriorated. To be blunt about it, for two years I was either pregnant or recovering from being pregnant – that is quite an emotional and physical battering for anyone to take, let alone a woman under vast amounts of work pressure.

It is no coincidence that after one last wake-up call, I decided that it was time to exit the organisation as well as start questioning the medics about my recurrent miscar- riages. I needed to give myself one last throw of the dice to become a mum before I turned forty, from a place of mental and physical calm. It is not a coincidence, because work and home are not disconnected... oh, yes, I know some people would have you believe the two are separate, but in my own lived experience and experience of working with men and women from all walks of life, the two are intrinsically linked.

Whether you show up in your jeans or in your suit, you are still driven by the same set of values, behaviours, motivations, and beliefs.

You get to choose one set of core values and they course direct all parts of your life.

KEEP CALM AND SET BOUNDARIES

"Boundaries are finding a way to be generous towards others while continuing to stay in your integrity."

— BRENE BROWN

Make no mistake, it was a bitter pill to acknowledge the fact that after being a rising star of the organisation my face no longer fitted. But this is a fact of life — whether it is business or personal. You grow and change with some organisations or relationships, and from others you grow apart. You do have a choice about how you react, behave, and think about that too. And it all starts with the boundaries you choose to put in place in your relationships.

The importance of boundaries was the biggest lesson I learnt during the first Covid-19 Lockdown in 2020. It was a huge turning point for me in my learnings about the boundary choices (or lack of) I made with friends and business acquaintances. After receiving a few metaphorical slaps to my face by people I'd invested my time, friendship and loyalty in (not to mention the cost investment of unpaid advice, training and intellectual capital), I realised I had to step up to the plate and acknowledge it was me who had made the poor choices, which, in part, had enabled this to happen. Another ouch moment. Why? Because I had made the choice to over-give and over-share like a mo-fo with zero boundaries in place. It was me who made the choice to give so much without setting out what I expected in return.

Over-helping and over-giving are very rarely rewarded with an equal response when the other person does not have equal skin in the game. Particularly when you have not given the other person a choice in the matter. And people without equal skin in the game rarely appreciate what they have been given on a silver platter, because they did not choose to ask for or receive it.

Choosing your Boundaries make everything in business and in friendships so much easier;

including our ability to say no with grace and humility.

THE SHIFT

"When a woman finally learns pleasing the world is impossible, she finally becomes free to learn how to please herself."

— GLENNON DOYLE

It was pretty apparent after the first few months of motherhood that my destiny was not to be a stay home Earth Mother. Hats off to those who are, but that is not my bag. I wanted to get back in the corporate saddle and get back to my money-earning ways, but without the ridiculous hours and the long commute. The phone rang a lot before I had my baby with job offers: why wouldn't it again?

There is nothing as deafening as a phone that does not ring when you want it to.

I said Hello to the spectre of unconscious prejudice against new mothers in the workplace... a confidence draining, identity dissolving, money reducing spectre of female disempowerment. Or so I told my angry, insulted, embarrassed self. It is true that prejudice exists, and it is also true that the glass ceiling is A Thing. But glass can be shattered by those who are courageous enough to choose to push on through.

I would like to say that I was that woman who took a battering ram to the ceiling; I had done it before. But not this time… I was too exhausted physically and emotionally, and not in the right mindset. Struggling to even get an interview, I reduced my expectations and standards rung by rung and eventually got a job I'd done a decade ago, earning less than half my previous salary in an educational organisation as a square peg in a round hole with no prospects.

I lasted less than six months. It was a terrible decision made again without really thinking through my choices. I had decided to make myself small based on the victim mentality, thinking I did not have a choice. I regretted my actions the day I first walked through the door. I was DONE with that world. I wanted out.

But more than this, I was admitting to myself I wanted to open my mind to new ways of thinking. And being. It was time to make the biggest choice of my professional life: to please myself.

So aged 42 I decided to retrain as a mature student. A week later I was enrolled on a Chinese Medicine Acupuncture degree course. I was a full time master's level student turning my back on my previous career and forging an entirely new identity for myself. No salary, no pension, no bonus, no company car, no paid holidays, no sick pay. And no guarantees.

But I was not making a random bet on a horse, I was taking a chance on myself.

I chose to pick up and start filling my Fuck It Bucket. And I haven't looked back since.

MONEY MATTERS

"Money is currency and currency is energy."

— JEN SINCERO

I want to make money from my profession, and I make no apologies for saying so. I am a businesswoman of considerable experience and I want to provide my services with skill, expertise, humility, integrity, and fairness and be paid the right amount of money in return. About six months into my degree I saw opportunities to do things differently in the wellbeing space before it became on-trend to talk about it. I saw how I could combine my business skills, my leadership skills, my person skills, my new therapy skills and create something totally different and totally value-adding to my prospective clients.

So yes… I opened my first clinic. A full-time student with no income of my own except savings, a toddler, a crazy dog, a home, a partner and all the other responsibilities of being an adult, but with the ambition to bring my vision to life. And with a whole lot of business acumen, self-belief and a Fuck It Bucket to fill, I made the choice to take a chance on myself, and I changed my future in this one decision.

My clinic was a beautifully decorated little room on a business park, which I opened with no clients and an empty Facebook page. Within twelve months I had outgrown this premises and moved to a bigger place in town.

With every month that goes by in my business, I realise that my potential lies beyond the boundaries of what someone else decides is appropriate. If you think small, you will get small. If you have courage and think big, you stand a good chance of being someone you never thought possible.

The only person who dictates your choice of thoughts is you.

FIND YOUR TRIBE

"Call it a Clan. Call it a Network. Call it a Tribe. Call it a Family. Whatever you call it, whoever you are, you need one."

— JANE HOWARD

Having led teams of people and then doing a 180 to fly solo as an entrepreneur in a completely different sector has brought it home how important it is for your wellbeing (and for your pocket) to have people around who you respect, like, know, trust and can learn from. None of us have all the answers to everything in life, however much of a guru you might be in your zone of genius, which is why you KNOW when you have eventually found your tribe; it is a visceral moment.

Humans are hard wired to belong in a community. You know you have arrived in your happy place when your community offers you a space where the unwritten rules of give and take are clear, nobody ends up disappointed or resentful, and most importantly your values are reflected in the behaviours and words of those around you.

If you ever wonder about the quality of your work relationships and whether people really are in your personal or professional tribe, a good measuring stick is the way people behave towards you when you are not there to speak for yourself. When I left my high paying corporate job through my own choice, my successor appeared to have made it his business to undermine my business skills, intellect, leadership, and achievements. The pinnacle of his combat exercise was a public execution of my reputation on a stage in front of hundreds of former colleagues, friends, and industry influencers. Those who identified an opportunity to rise up the ranks applauded, whilst those who knew differently voted with their feet. However, instead of getting mad or sad, I chose to use this as a way of deciding who I wanted in my life, who I wanted to be as a person. And not be.

Equally, we should not avoid having critics in our tribe… but make sure they are critical friends. There is a difference. Brene Brown nailed it in one powerful statement when she talked about the critics who throw around their views and opinions whilst sitting in the cheapest seats of the arena, watching the show: "IF YOU ARE NOT IN THE ARENA I'M NOT INTERESTED IN YOUR FEEDBACK."

That hit me right between the eyes. Why? Because not only do I have a profession which divides opinion on whether it is scientific or medical "enough" to be taken seriously (by standards set against a different paradigm), I am a forty-something year old woman who shows up as myself in the gladiatorial arena of social media.

Both reasons are enough to attract the critics. Even my sister has defended my profession to two self-described scientists and an accountant. And I have been trolled a few times over various things, none of whom are slogging it out in the arena with me. They are sitting in the cheap seats, shouting the loudest boos. And therefore, I am not interested in their opinions.

In contrast, your Tribe will support you, challenge you and pick you up when you fall. Having a tribe means you do not always have to be strong - as someone with a huge "be strong" driver this is a big deal. It is not the quantity of the company you keep; it is the quality which makes you happy, fulfilled and making money on the terms you want to make it.

Having a tribe allows you to have other people in your life that want to love and nurture you, but you need to make the choice to allow them to do so.

OWN WHO YOU ARE

"Everything in the universe is within you. Ask all from yourself."

— RUMI

Sounds easy. Just be yourself. Until you must start being yourself on social media, with potential clients, in front of your competitors. Then the whole itty-bitty-shitty imposter committee sitting on your shoulder starts pecking your head.

Ignore it. Think about your Fuck It Bucket and know this:

- It takes courage to show up as yourself day in day out.
- It takes acceptance of one's vulnerability to know there will always be naysayers and critics and carry on regardless.
- You also have your supporters - which includes the critical friend and the ones you are helping.

As we go through tough times it is tempting to hide away. Or pretend to be someone we are not. Or go to the default option of making ourselves small.

Don't.

Choose Yourself.

ABOUT THE AUTHOR

Kate Morris-Bates

Kate is a straight-talking, practical wellness expert on a mission to help 40+ women take control of their bodies and minds.

She is the founder of InsideOut Wellness Centre in North Wales; a former corporate high flyer who is now one of very few post-graduate degree qualified Chinese Medicine Acupuncture practitioners in the UK; and a certified CBT (cognitive behaviour therapy) coach, qualified in body therapy and medical skin treatments and a specialist in alternative approaches to pain management.

Kate is passionate about using her two decades of professional and lived experience to support 40+ women to stand in their power, putting themselves first and living their best lives, in the body they have.

As a successful entrepreneur, Kate's story has been published in two books about Inspiring Women and has spoken about women's health and wellness on public stages across the UK.

Her clients include individuals from across the spectrum of society – business owners, scientists, surgeons, executive mums, care workers, retired women and more.

Her mission is to provide her clients with tailor made individual wellness support by fusing Eastern and Western philosophies to health and wellbeing so they can stand confidently in their power and show up as their best selves every single day.

CONTACT:

EMAIL: mailto:kate@katemorrisbates.com
WEBSITE: https://katemorrisbates.com/
FACEBOOK: https://www.facebook.com/
groups/wellbeinglounge

instagram.com/katemorrisbates_wellness
linkedin.com/in/katemorris-bates-wellness-expert

KERRY ASHBY

It is just a midlife crisis

Sat here with a cuppa I am reflecting on how my life has changed and – holy moly – has it changed!

I am happy, content and a million miles away from where I was in my other life; I am not talking about past life regression, I am talking about my other life in the corporate world: my successful but stressful life and a life I walked away from on my 50th birthday whilst sat on a sunbed on the beach in Mexico.

It did not happen by chance, or overnight. It was a long time coming although I did not realise it at the time. What did happen on my 50th birthday was the realisation that I couldn't go on doing what I was doing; I needed to change my life and I was the only person who could do it.

So I turned my back on that life. The perfect life that everyone told me I was so lucky to have, that life that took everything from me, dragged me down and nearly tipped me over the edge.

Looking back, I realise that I should have done it years before, but hindsight is a wonderful thing. I am just so grateful that I did it. I am now happier than ever, and my new life is helping others to achieve the life and business that they will love and deserve.

By sharing my story I want to show you that if I can do this, so can you. Sometimes you need to be brave, put on those big girl pants and follow your heart. We all have dreams and aspirations, but we can all turn these into reality? Yes, we bloody well can!

BURN OUT IS REAL

The look in my manager's eyes said it all! What are you thinking? Are you crazy? The unspoken word was so powerful, I could tell what she was thinking and part of me believed this was true too. I was leaving the job I had worked twenty years to achieve.

Unfortunately, it was not just my manager that reacted like this. I knew that friends felt the same and my mum was horrified. I kept hearing the same comments: 'Why would you give up everything you have worked for?... But you are a nurse, how can you give up a career to play with flowers?' and, 'I hope you get this out of your system quickly,' and, 'It's just a midlife crisis.'

Burnout is real and it was happening to me, the person that looked after everyone else. I could not stop crying and I was so tired I was barely functioning. But something amazing came out of this horrendous situation. I was given some precious time, time to reflect, time to re-evaluate my life and ultimately make decisions. So it turned out it was not in fact a midlife crisis but the best decision I could have made for the sake of my sanity and my life.

I left school at sixteen and had a few jobs but never really found my 'thing'. But I knew once I found it, that would be it. I went to college and got a qualification in health and social care, got bored and left! I worked as a nanny, got bored and left! I worked in a flower shop, got bored and left! You can see the pattern here: start something, get bored and leave, and I never really found that thing that put the fire in my belly and gave me something to get up for. So I kept looking.

During this time, I got married (did not get bored, and have not left!) I had three beautiful and amazing children, Sophie, Josh, and Alice, and I loved being a mum. But I knew I never wanted to be **that** mum that stayed at home and chatted at the school gates. I wanted to work doing something challenging and worthwhile. I decided that when Alice, my youngest, was born I needed to find that thing I was looking for, that thing that would give me something to focus on. So what did I do? I went to university.

At thirty, university was an eye opener. I had not studied since I was sixteen and did not even have a computer back then, but here I was as a mature student walking into the University of Hertfordshire about to start my training. I was going to be a nurse.

Was it hard? Yes, it bloody was! I was on a three-year course and I had to juggle studying, work placements and three children with the youngest only ten months old. I was not in any way technical and had no idea how to use a computer. But I did it. I qualified as a paediatric nurse after three exceptionally long years and finally had a career and not just a job.

I never intended to be anything other than a nurse after that. I got my dream job in Accident and Emergency and loved it. I was working hard, learning loads, and felt I was making a difference. It was stressful and not something I could have done for ever: I witnessed death on a daily basis and that's hard to comprehend, but we laughed loads too and I will always be grateful for that time. It made me realise that life is very precious, and we should not waste it. I will come back to this thought later.

WORKING MY WAY UP

I never planned to go into management, that just kind of happened. Staff nurse, senior staff nurse, and then I became a sister quite quickly. It meant added responsibilities, but I enjoyed it, it kept me busy and I loved mentoring the students and junior staff.

I really enjoyed taking them from a worried, sometimes scared newbie to someone who I could see growing in confidence and skills every day. This was something I always hoped would continue throughout my career and it is what I do now but in my other life.

The hours and stress of A&E took its toll and after a few years of working Christmas Day, nights and twelve hour shifts I decided the time was right to move on when I was, out of the blue, offered a Monday to Friday job in the private sector. I had always worked for the NHS but decided it was too good an opportunity to give up and I went for it.

I found myself working for a company that specialised in home infusions for children with life limiting conditions and I loved it. Because the conditions were ultra-rare, I found myself driving up and down the country administering infusions. I was generally happy. I did this for a couple of years until management changed and the job did too, so I needed to do something else.

I updated my CV and put it online and within twenty minutes was offered an interview. Now this was in an arena that I knew nothing about – mental health. Eating disorders, specifically. It was a topic that I knew nothing about but decided to go for it and got offered the job. This was the start of my management path.

'I would like to offer you the job of team leader,' they said. Gulp… I wasn't expecting that! But I thought *I'm more than capable* so before I realised it I had accepted and the ball was rolling.

I started with a small team and loved it. In fact, I stayed there for a couple of years. It was easy and I got a lot of job satisfaction, and then I got a call…

'Something that will interest you'

'… Kerry, we have heard about you and we have a position that we would love you to consider. We really think this is something that will interest you.' *Hmm, ok, tell me more,* I thought.

That is how I became a ward manager for a competitor. Another eating disorder unit had opened and it was brand new. They wanted me to join them.

This job was really challenging, but it gave me something to get my teeth into and gave me so much more management experience. I found myself managing a large team of nurses and health care workers in a secure unit.

I could do the management side but as a paediatric nurse and not mental health trained, I was always the odd one out. I could do the medical stuff easily, took blood and cannulated with ease, ECGs were no problem, but I was honest with them and never really understood the mental health side the way others did. This worked because we balanced each other out. Everyone was mental health trained, the unit was managed by psychiatrists and they were happy with my medical background, so I got involved in everything and with everyone. But because I was the only medic amongst a huge team I was always in demand, often getting calls at the weekend asking me about blood results and ECGs. This was not ideal, and it took its toll.

Once again out of the blue I got a call.

Yes, it was that call!

'Kerry, we wanted to speak to you because we have something you may be interested in…'

Here we go again – but this did interest me because it was from the same company that I had worked for a couple of jobs back, the job I loved until the management changed, the job that was Monday to Friday. So I thought, *Ok, tell me more.*

WHAT YOU HAVE BEEN WAITING FOR

'We want to talk to you about a management position that we think you are perfect for!' they said.

I was sceptical because I knew the management structure was wobbly to say the least. That was, of course, why I left, so I listened and was interested in what had changed, if anything.

Well, it turned out quite a lot had changed, in fact. The company I had left had since been bought out and they were now a little cog in a bigger wheel. Well, they were not really that little and that is why they wanted to talk to me.

'Kerry, we want to speak to you about becoming our Paediatric Manager. We think this job is perfect for you and just what you have been waiting for.'

I was sceptical to say the least but agreed to go for an 'informal chat'. I didn't even really want the job so wasn't going straight into an interview so found myself trudging through the snow along the M1 one January morning. Cold and not in the best of moods, I pitched up in Northampton already convincing myself I did not want this, but I was wrong.

I did listen to what they had to say, and I did in fact want this, desperately wanted this. So I told them that and told them I wanted an interview. It happened, and I started work four weeks later.

I really enjoyed this job and would most probably still be doing it now if things had not changed so drastically.

I was managing a lovely team. It was a national team and hard work at times, but I had a good handle on it. It was the perfect mix of being customer focused (my customers being the NHS paediatric hospital metabolic departments), managing a lovely team of paediatric nurses and still occasionally doing hands on nursing. I could keep up my skills and things were good for six months.

THAT MEETING WHERE EVERYTHING CHANGED

I was at the office doing a stock take, bored and ridiculously hot. It was the summer and I was in a room with lots of windows and very little air when my manager came in. Nothing unusual about that and said I needed to attend a meeting in her place as she was going on holiday the next day. I did not question it at the time, but I remember thinking, if I am driving all the way to Northampton again tomorrow to talk about stock, I will not be happy. How wrong I was!

I was early so grabbed a cuppa and sat in the board room. It didn't occur to me that something big was going to happen, even when the room filled up with all the other heads of departments and I was still a little peeved that I had driven to Northampton for a 4pm meeting.

'There is no easy way to say this, so I am just going to read out a statement,' they said. And then it happened. 'We have been trying to sell the business for a while, blah blah blah, and have not been able to do so, therefore we have no option but to close.'

WTF! How could this be happening? I had left a secure job six months before and this was going on behind the scenes.

I had two days that I had to keep this to myself because the announcement was coming on Friday. That was a miserable time. I had to carry on as normal knowing that my whole team were at risk. Friday came and what a day! Lots of tears and questions and I had never looked forward to a weekend like I looked forward to that weekend.

Fast forward a couple of weeks and we got a lifeline, or so I thought at the time.

'Kerry, good news. The whole service is being moved to a competitor and you are all moving with it. Get ready to TUPE.'

AND THE STRESS STARTS

The job itself was the same, the same team, and the same role, but for a much bigger company. This company was a household name. They were the big boys, and they saw an opportunity to grab a specialised established service, including the specialist staff and a full patient caseload that was missing from their portfolio of services, and they took the contract, staff, and all.

That was how I ended up in a job that caused me to burn out.

Life was crazy. I found myself managing a team that spanned from Aberdeen to Jersey and every children's hospital in between. I was on first name terms with reception staff at many Premier Inns which probably showed that I was away from home too much.

I was tired, or so I thought! I was working up to sixty hours a week and spent at least three nights away from home. My week usually started on Monday with an early morning flight to Scotland and because the flight home every single week was delayed, I did not usually get home until midnight. Tuesday I could be in Birmingham or Manchester and Wednesday in London, so you get the picture. Life was not as easy as it once was and I was not only keeping my company happy I was trying to keep five NHS trusts and a large team of nurses happy, single handed.

I kept asking for help but kept being told, 'It's ok, you're doing a good job,' but I was struggling.

SHOVE YOUR JOB

It all came to a head one sunny day in September. I remember it well although it was a day I would like to forget. It was a Tuesday and Monday had been the day from hell. I had flown to Glasgow for a meeting that was cancelled, but nobody thought to tell me! My flight was delayed as usual and then, even worse, cancelled. I had the choice to stay in Glasgow or fly to Heathrow. I chose Heathrow so got home at 1am both miserable and tired.

I woke up early because I had a meeting in Birmingham, I had a headache and was tearful but put it down to being tired. I drove to Birmingham, had a terrible meeting where they complained about everything and I drove home. I pulled up onto the drive and the phone rang. It was our HR department. I said *hello* and did not even get a hello back. What I got was, 'Kerry, I asked you for your report yesterday. You have not sent it. Can you explain why?' At that moment I lost it. I mean, really lost it! I exploded and told her that she could shove their job.

Well, that opened a can of worms they were not expecting. I turned off my car and phone and went into the house and cried. Not just a quick emotional sob, I really cried, and this went on for hours. I cried all evening and most of the night. I knew something was not right but still at that time thought I was tired.

I finally fell asleep and woke up with the worst headache ever. I took some paracetamol and went back to sleep. I did not turn my phone back on.

I slept and cried for days but could not think straight. I did not know what to do but knew something had to change. I could not go on like this.

I was so tired but thankfully was going on a much-needed holiday in two weeks' time. It was my 50th birthday so I had booked two weeks in Mexico, all inclusive, upgraded to VIP section, the works. I decided that I would go to the GP and get myself signed off for a couple of weeks, go on holiday, relax and refresh, and go back to work. That was the plan.

MY LIFE CHANGED AT THAT POINT

Fast forward a couple of weeks and I was sat on a beautiful Balinese bed on the beach in Mexico and life should have been good, but it was not. I was on anti-depressants, exhausted and burnt out. It was on that bed that I decided I needed to make a life changing move that was going to have a huge impact on my life.

"Paul, I am not going back to work," I blurted out, not quite sure what I was expecting him to say, but he just said, " I don't blame you, you should have left before now," so that was that, decision made on a bed on the beach in Mexico. Now I would love to say that I had the holiday of a lifetime, but I did not, I spent most of it asleep or crying.

I reflected on my time in A&E and it reminded me how precious life was, how easily things can change and in an instant life can be taken away. Working in an environment where life can be extinguished in a blink of an eye made me realise it's now or never.

I would be interested in your thoughts right now. Do you recognise any of the symptoms of burnout in yourself? You have the power to make a choice to change things so don't worry about what others think. Your life and your happiness is what is important; don't forget this and don't forget YOU!

I came home and handed my notice in, but I had no intention of working it. I got myself signed off again. Now this was not something I enjoyed doing; I had only ever had a couple of days off sick in twenty years.

What could I do now? *I know, I will start my own business!* I thought.

YOU DO NOT KNOW WHAT YOU DO NOT KNOW

And that was what I did. I started my own business. I had no idea how to launch a business let alone run a business, but I just had a go. Not the best way to start a business but I did not know what I did not know!

'I am going to be a florist.' That sounded like a great idea when I announced it. It was a lot harder than it sounded.

I got myself booked on a weeklong intensive course to learn some new techniques; things had moved on in the twenty years since I left the flower shop that I worked in.

I knew I had made the right decision; I loved every minute and my mind was made up; I was going to specialise in weddings.

I still had bills to pay so decided to go back to nursing, part time and as a nurse, not a manager. This allowed me to build my business whilst still bringing some money in.

Where to start? Now that was a million-dollar question and I did not have a clue. Not a single clue. I asked some friends; they did not have a clue either, so I just started. I thought of a business name that was ok… well, it was a bit rubbish, but I did not know the importance of it back then like I do now.

My daughter's friend said she could build me a website. Great, that was something ticked off the list and it made me feel like a real business. Right now, to get some work!

I posted some photos on Facebook and got loads of enquiries, I remember thinking, 'This is going to be easy!' How wrong that thought was.

I needed somewhere to work so I bought myself a work-shop in the garden. Now when I say workshop, what I mean is quite a large shed, but I loved it. Not only did I have a website I now had a workshop which I decided I would call a studio because I thought it sounded better.

I had my studio and enquiries so needed to convert these to bookings. Which I did very easily, but what I did not realise at the time was that this was going to backfire quite dramatically, and I would be terribly busy but not making any money at all. Not a penny and I was going to have to continue nursing to subsidise my business.

Fast forward to now and I can see this was the wrong approach. Little did I know back then that my business today would be based on the mistakes I made.

It took me around a year to realise something was wrong. I did not want to go back to nursing full time, I did not even want to work part time. I wanted to work on my business, not in somebody else's. Something had to change. I got advice from a business coach and it changed my life!

I know that is quite a bold statement, but it really did. The first thing she asked me was who was my ideal client? I didn't know I needed one, let alone know who they were. The second thing she asked me was what did I want my business to look like? I just looked blank and said I had no idea.

I turned my business around; I went from naively thinking I could run a business to really running a business, getting booked with couples that wanted me to work with them. I upped my prices and made a profit.

I want to do that too!

'Can you teach me?' I was not expecting to be asked that, but then I thought why not? So that is how my second business started. If I can do it then why can't others?

I set up a flower school with the intention of teaching both practical floristry and business in equal measures and it went really well, better than I expected if I am honest and I loved teaching again.

I belonged to a few floristry Facebook groups and was surprised at how unhelpful they were, especially to new self-taught or bench trained florists. That annoyed me. Everyone needs a safe space to ask questions because I knew first-hand that we do not know what we do not know.

I started a Facebook group and had no idea that would change my business model once again.

I was still doing weddings but getting more and more requests to help florists with their businesses... I was struggling to fit everything in. I loved weddings but loved helping others more.

Over the past year things have changed and I made another big decision. I was going to sell my wedding business and focus on helping others.

I knew instantly that this was the right decision; that is what I did and that is what brings me here today.

I now use my experience, my bad decisions, and my lack of knowledge to help others. I completely agree in collaboration over competition and have made it my mission to help as many florists as I possibly can to launch and grow a successful floristry career.

I love nothing better than telling them about my mistakes and how to avoid them. I still make mistakes but now I use them to teach others. I now have a business that is me, unapologetically me and I have nothing to hide behind! No flowers, no pretty venues, just me and I love it. I have never been happier.

So as I sit here with that cuppa, reflecting on how my life has changed and I look back to that person sat on the sunbed crying in Mexico, I am grateful for that time because had I not burnt out, I would not be here now doing something I love and something that helps so many people, not just me.

Do not ever think you are too old to start your own business. Do not tell yourself you cannot do this and do not listen to those naysayers! You can absolutely do this; you are not crazy. So, believe in yourself, put on your big girl pants and go for it! Do not regret trying and if I can do it you can do it too.

ABOUT THE AUTHOR

Kerry Ashby

Kerry Ashby is a straight talking, creative business coach, empowering florists to rebel against the stereotypes, break the mould and do things differently.

Kerry is passionate about sharing her business knowledge, work experience and creative expertise to help others thrive in their life, business and career. She encourages clients to focus on themselves and have the confidence to build the business they have always wanted but never thought they could have.

Having changed career at fifty she understands the struggles and self-doubt that creep in, and her mission is to help as many florists as possible succeed in business using the tools, skills and strategies that have helped her create a variety of successful businesses not only for herself, but for so many of her clients too.

With a strong belief in collaboration over competition, Kerry gives her advice freely to those starting out in the world of floristry and can often be found in her free Facebook group Business in Bloom.

Kerry is also the proud founder of The Rebel Florist Club, a powerful collaboration of like-minded and aspirational florists in a membership with the sole purpose to bring quality coaching and support to those determined to leave the stereotypes behind, rip up the rulebook, and ready to kick ass.

CONTACT:

EMAIL:
Kerry@kerryashbycoaching.com
WEBSITE:
https://kerryashbycoaching.com
FACEBOOK:
https://www.facebook.com/groups/therebelfloristclub/
https://www.facebook.com/
groups/HFSbusinessinbloom/

facebook.com/kerryashbycoaching

instagram.com/kerryashbycoaching

12

KIMBERLEY WHITTALL-MALLOCH

Who do you think you are?

In July 2010, I lay on a bed with beeping noises all around me and wires coming out of everywhere. All I could see was several dwarf-like characters covered in mousy brown hair from top to bottom resembling the character Itt – you know, the hairy one out of the Addams Family.

I was tripping, tripping my tits off on all the diamorphine and the concoction of other drugs the doctors had given me.

I'd gone into hospital for a routine operation that had gone a bit wrong- to say the least! After the op I appeared ok and got sent home the next day. That evening I was getting into bed and this pain started. I thought, it's ok I'm used to pain, I can manage this, it'll subside... but it didn't, it got more intense and then even more intense. It was in my chest area and it started to spread down my left arm. I thought, Holy shit, am I having some kind of heart attack? The pain worsened and I said to my (now) husband (who you could see was trying to be calm but he had that shitting himself look behind the eyes), "I think you need to call an ambulance."

The ambulance arrived, the paramedics tried to calm me down but the pain was just too intense so they gave me a shot of morphine which took the edge off a tad. I arrived at the hospital, was rolled in on a bed and left in the corridor, then the immense pain kicked back in. I was a blubbering mess and was told to be quiet. I'm no wimp and I have quite a high pain threshold, or did more so back then. They eventually took me for an ECG which showed no signs of a heart attack (phew). Ok, so what was all the pain about?

They transferred me to another ward… the staff were confused as to what was wrong. They thought it was trapped gas from having the keyhole surgery, as they blew you up like a balloon with gas to do the operation. They suggested that I drink something fizzy, so I drank a can of coke… which I hate, but I was desperate. I would have drunk petrol at that point if I knew it was going to help the pain. They also suggested peppermint tea (I still have flashbacks when I smell peppermint tea). Their theory was that the fizzy drinks would help release some gas and the peppermint tea would settle my stomach.

My intuition was that it was utter bullshit and some kind of pacifier. Something was seriously wrong and I knew it, but I couldn't get through to them. I actually think they thought I was being dramatic. Anyway, so I drank the bloody tea and fizzy drinks which made the pain a million times worse. I'd closed the curtains around my bed and I was lucky to have a wall next to me so I would put my hands on the wall like I was doing some pushups against it to try and push against the wall and breathe through the pain. Honestly, it was like labour on steroids, so much so that when my now husband would come and visit me, I would tell him to go after ten minutes; I didn't have the brain power to converse. I was using all my mental energy on getting through the pain.

After a few days of lots of morphine and pain they took me down to have a camera put into my stomach to see what was going on. They sedated me and all I can remember is them trying to put the camera down my throat and my body was just rejecting it. I couldn't control it, it just wouldn't stay down in my stomach, so they knew something wasn't right. They wheeled me back to the ward and took my bloods again and my results came back later that day, which is when a surgeon came to see me and tell me that my organs had started to fail (I was feeling rather unwell at this point). They rushed me to emergency surgery; something was definitely up to no good in my stomach area.

They took me down to surgery at around 8am the next morning, anesthetized me and they went all in.

I'll spare you the details.

Let me tell you where the pain was coming from... bile, which is acid that breaks down your food from your liver. Imagine that someone threw acid on you and it hit your skin: it would burn and scar. Well, this is what was being pumped into all my insides for six days. That is why drinking coke and peppermint tea somehow didn't solve the problem. That is why when they tried to put a camera into my stomach my body rejected it.

My body was saying, no thanks, I'm trying to deal with what's going on in here already.

It took over seven hours to repair what had happened in there, umpteen doctors scratching their heads and an emergency call to a liver specialist in a different hospital to come and help out... fortunately he was on site. Someone was looking down on me that day for sure.

And that's when I woke up with all the wires and the Itt like characters around my bed in a high dependency unit.

It was very surreal. I felt so calm considering what I'd just been through (pretty sure the constant pump of diamorphine was partly something to do with it). Although there was something else. I had this new meaning to life, death and being a human. I remember my breathing was very shallow (my oxygen saturation levels were quite low) and I had an oxygen mask on that kept slipping off and the nurse kept saying to me I had to keep it on otherwise I'd end up in critical care on a ventilator. It was strange because the thought of slipping away didn't scare me even though I was only 27 years old.

Here's the woo bit... I don't know why to this day, but I knew there was something else beyond the physical realm that was supporting me. I can't fully explain it. It was just a deep knowing. I felt so calm and grateful to be alive, like I'd been given another opportunity to live life. All the menial things that used to bother me seemed to fade away and I felt this sense of pure love. This is when I knew I had a purpose in life and I just had to discover it fully.

I spent a week or so in the high dependency unit, getting high off the morphine with a press of a button, being bathed in bed, peeing into bags and watching Brokeback Mountain.

I was transferred to another ward after a week or so where I could start going to the toilet for myself and was allowed shakes and soft food. I couldn't eat soup for several years. Even several years later I would still have flashbacks when I saw and smelt soup. The days would all mould into one: drink shakes, eat soft food, go for a pee, get high off the morphine, watch trailer trash, family would visit, fall asleep and dream weird shit.

I was itching to get the hell out of the hospital. A few weeks passed and I was set free. I was elated, grinning from ear to ear! I couldn't wait to get home and spend time with my daughter, partner and see family and friends and sleep in my own bed.

My partner came to pick me up, I was ready, packed and waiting to go. Then we got the go ahead to go home. I remember being so happy in the car, cracking jokes, being grateful to be alive and noticing everything around me – the trees, the birds, people walking by. It was like I was experiencing life for the first time, like a baby first experiencing life.

I was totally present in that moment.

We arrived home, my partner picked our daughter up from nursery and we had lots of gentle cuddles and tears (from me) on the couch. I was so happy to be back together as a family. I stayed in that feeling of gratitude for a while.

My cousin suggested that I read the book *The Secret*, so I did. What I read opened up my eyes to a new way of thinking and how we can work with the universe. I was so intrigued. This was the time I first started dabbling in personal development.

I started buying the magazine psychologies and ditched all those celebrity gossip magazines that actually either make you feel like shit or make others look like shit. My employer at the time suggested seeing a life coach whom she recommended, so we did. We wanted to get our lives back on track and we were open to anything.

Just to give some background, during the nine months before this major surgery, we had encountered a string of events... we found out we were victims of fraud by a "family member" and only found out when the police knocked at our door. A few days following this my daughter developed epilepsy literally overnight after having a nasty virus. It took us several months of seizures and very little sleep in that time for her to become stable on medication. My mum was also hospitalised for several months through this time too. The major surgery was like the icing on a shit cake.

But I was determined to stay positive. I was actually a bit of an expert in pretending everything was ok. I had many years of practice in my childhood and young adult years.

There's a thing about staying positive – it works really well, but only when you've truly dealt with the shitstorms that have actually traumatised you. Otherwise it's just like sticking a plaster on an infected wound and it will hit you at some point. Sometimes it will rear its head in self sabo-tage with food, alcohol, relationships and money. The wound will find its way to leak out into different parts of your life. Until you heal it. Starting my own personal journey with Coaching, NLP and then Rapid Transfor-mational Therapy transformed my mindset. It gave me the time and permission to heal and to see the world through a different lens than ever before. I could be, do and have anything I wanted. All I had to do was change the meanings of the shitty experiences and create my new life going forwards.

Being physically out of action for several months… being unable to exercise, or to pick your child up, or to drive, really makes you really appreciate the seemingly small things like going for a walk, putting your child into their car seat, doing the food shopping and lifting up a kettle to make your friend a brew.

So as soon as I was able to gain some normality back and was able to drive again, I went back to uni at the end of September 2010 to complete my second year in Event Management. It was great to get back to what I enjoyed learning. Yes, it was uncomfortable to sit in one position at a desk for periods of time. It was painful to laugh, cough and I flinched every time someone came too close to me, but it was worth it to just be around my friends again. Unfortunately, I couldn't return to work yet. I worked in Event Management at the time and that would have been too much to take on.

Fast forward several months

I found myself pregnant with my second daughter, which was a miracle. I was finishing my exams, the dream house we were renting and were once planning to buy was being sold so we had to find somewhere new. One of my best friends who lived in Cheltenham said, 'Come and move here.' So we did.

We settled in well in Cheltenham. My neighbour turned into one of my best friends to date.

I had my youngest beautiful daughter in November 2011. Three weeks later had my appendix out (another near miss and misdiagnosis) and again recovered, pretending I was ok. Another big scar; why not add to the collection?

This was literally my life. All through my life there was always something…

I became desensitised to it, almost expecting something to happen on an unconscious level.

This is not a great message to send out to the universe. In fact, I was unintentionally sending out a lot of mixed messages to the universe. Consciously I was wanting to create a new life: I was writing out my goals, being grateful, being aware of the mental chatter and changing it. Subconsciously I was still on high alert for something to happen. This is one example of sending out mixed messages to the universe. The universe listens to both the conscious and unconscious and gets confused. It doesn't know what to send you. So funnily enough good things would happen but then not so good things would happen (the timing was impeccable) which would totally tarnish the good stuff.

As life went on things seemed to settle down. We were getting back on track with finances, I was losing baby weight and my desire and excitement to go back to work was growing. So, with that in mind we decided to move back up north to a quaint village called Great Budworth in Cheshire in the summer of 2013, where we would be closer to family and helping hands if we needed it while our girls were still young.

The help was needed much sooner than we thought. As I was losing weight a part of my stomach was growing... Nope not pregnant. I had a huge incisional hernia from the major surgery. Yes, another operation needed! Luckily this time they managed to do it by keyhole, which was pretty impressive as they put a big piece of mesh in there instead of closing up the holes as that doesn't always work so well.

Right, seriously this had to be it now.

The universe had actually delivered to me the unconscious high alert stuff that was going on in my subconscious. We are always manifesting — the good, the bad and the ugly.

Things were looking up. I was headhunted and offered a great job back in the dental world which was my industry before event management. So I took the job.

Everything on paper looked great. We were renting a big new house in a gorgeous little village, my oldest went to the local village school and my youngest went to a gorgeous nursery. I bought a new car, we met new friends and my job was going well. I felt independent again. Several months passed.

Then I started to become very unsettled. My relationship with my partner became quite distant. Cracks started to appear. I started to question a lot of whether we should even be together. I felt disconnected from him. I felt I wanted more, but I didn't know what more really was? Like I said, everything looked great on "paper" and from an outsider's perspective, it was confusing.

All those life events that we'd been through together had taken their toll on our relationship. At the time we just got on with it but we didn't really talk things through at length and reflect. But there was more to it than that.

I was well and truly disconnected from myself. Who the fuck even was I? I'd completely lost myself in the shit-storms of events and to be honest looking back I think I'd always struggled to know who I really was for a long time and what I was really meant to do with my life.

This is common for kids that have experienced trauma.

I actually questioned if I could ever be truly happy. I even said to a couple of friends after quite a few wines that I didn't think I could ever be truly happy, because I just ruin it.

I was so used to having trauma after trauma all through my life and when there was nothing traumatic going on to deal with, it was almost like my subconscious was like... 'Woah, what's going on? This isn't right. I think we need to fuck something up just so we can feel that level of stress that's familiar.'

Our brains like familiarity and when something is not familiar (including stress) our brains will search for ways to find familiarity.

So that's exactly what my brain did... I pressed the self-destruct button.

I honestly thought that something was really wrong with me. I thought I had ADHD. I thought, 'Am I bipolar? What if I've got some kind of brain injury that's making me do crazy stuff?'

As it turned out, I had PTSD. The collection of traumas all the way from being a kid to nearly thirty years old had stacked up like a tower of Jenga and the last pieces were more than the tower could handle.

I saw a therapist who did some EMDR on me, then a counsellor and then a life coach.

The life coach asked me what I wanted. I said to be happy. That was my ultimate goal in life. To find my purpose and that is when my life started to change.

After working with my coach I began to see the world through a different lens. My perspectives changed. I knew

I was so much more in control of my thoughts and actions than I had ever thought before. This was the very start of my own transformation.

I started to revisit the thought of becoming a coach myself. This was something that I'd wanted to do after seeing my first coach around five years before, but at that time I didn't think anyone would take me seriously because I was under thirty, even though I'd experienced more than some people experience in a lifetime. I had quite a few limiting beliefs.

I had received some money as compensation from the major surgery fuck up and instead of spending the money on furniture and cosmetic surgery to reduce the scars, I decided to invest it in my own personal development and heal the internal scars, and then pay for the training to become a Transformational Coach and Rapid Transformational Therapist.

I completed six different qualifications in Transformational Coaching in Money, Health, Mindset, Business, Personality Profiling and Rapid Transformational Therapy. Plus two more qualifications which are ongoing.

While I was learning I was noticing I definitely had more work to do on myself , which is what I did. I peeled even more layers back and got to the root cause of what was truly holding me back from the success I wanted to achieve in my own business. Once I did that there was no stopping me, no imposter and no self-sabotage. I'm not saying I'm perfect and I'll always be a work in progress but I love that I can own that now and still be successful.

Now I am living the dream by helping my clients transform their lives with my five layer unique SPEED method, overcoming their blocks to success, such as unworthiness, self-sabotage, imposter syndrome, confidence, manifestation and business creation. I help them heal the stuff that's been holding them back on an unconscious level, helping them to reach their true potential in life and live the life they dream of with the freedom they desire.

On the subject of success, what does it REALLY mean to you? Because it's all relative: we all have different ideas of success.

For some it's having a million pounds in the bank; for others it's feeling financially comfortable. For some it's travelling the world; for others it's having a holiday home. For some it's freedom; for others it's stability. For some it's building an empire; for others it's working alone. For some it's taking big risks; for others it's creating security. For some it's life experiences; for others it's material things. For some it's impact and recognition; for others it's respect and appreciation.

Of course, we can have a blend of these desires and it's not always one or the other. It's just important that you believe you really can have what you want and what you want is available to you. This is a success in itself.

Do not let anyone ever tell you otherwise, including yourself.

My own idea of success is making a positive impact on as many people as possible while living life to the fullest with my family and friends, having happy children, living in a beautiful country near the sea, and travelling the world.

Success is an inside job.

Don't let your past define you. Every single one of my traumas has made me the person who I am today and I'm actually grateful for all the shit I've had to overcome because it was leading me to my purpose in life – but all those things that happened in the past do not define me. I decide who I want to be.

If you get triggered by something it's a sign that you need to heal and deal with it. Don't let it run your life and stop you making progress. Get to the root cause of the trigger, face it head on like a warrior, heal it and transform it.

Your pain can turn out to be your passion

It's funny how the little Kimberley who didn't like her voice because other people made comments on it belonging to a child (I didn't get into choir in primary school because my voice was too "low"). Now my voice is part of my superpower. I'm now forever being given compliments on my voice and my voice is what helps transform people.

I was told I was average at school at quite a young age, never putting my hand up in class with the fear I would get the answer wrong. Now I have multiple qualifications and a degree and I now I ask people questions for a living. Now I can put my hand on my heart and say I truly know what I'm here to do.

Don't undermine what you have succeeded at in life so far. My actual biggest achievement is my own unique qualification of my own life. As Oprah once said, "Turn your wounds into your wisdom."

You CAN change your programming and break patterns that are not serving you. You are not contracted to your old beliefs.

You are WORTHY of all the success you desire and it IS available to you.

Life is too bloody short not to take risks, live in the moment, have fun, experience all you want to experience and chase and catch your dreams.

We've just left the UK to live in Ibiza to catch ours... See you on the other side.

ABOUT THE AUTHOR

Kimberley Whittall-Malloch

Kimberley is a global coach and therapist with several qualifications in transformation, business, health and performance and has worked with startups to multi six figure entrepreneurs.

Over the past twenty years Kimberley has developed a wealth of experience in patient care in the private sector, as well as sales, training, marketing and business development for leading brands working B2B. She also spent several years working with high profile clients as an event manager in the events industry before following her calling to coaching.

Kimberley believes it is her life's purpose to help transform people from the inside out, having done this with her own life experiences. She runs a successful business and has now relocated with her husband and their two girls from Manchester in the UK to Ibiza to follow their dreams, where she will be running Wealth Success Retreats for entrepreneurs and corporates and continuing to transform her clients' mindsets for success either working 1:1 or in small groups.

It is Kimberley's mission to positively impact as many people's lives as possible and show them they can have what they desire and create a life of wealth and freedom.

Kimberley works with clients using her unique five layer Wealth SPEED Method. Her approach is holistic with a dash of strategy and rapid in terms of results. Kimberley works on a deep subconscious level to help her clients break free from any blocks that are holding them back from their success and helps them design a business which is in true alignment to who they are and what they truly want with ease and flow.

CONTACT:

Email:
kimberley@wealthandworthcatalyst.com
Website
www.wealthandworthcatalyst.com

facebook.com/kimberleywhittallmalloch

instagram.com/wealthandworthcatalyst

linkedin.com/in/kimberley-whittall-malloch-6a36b229

13

LAURA NAZIR

Confidence is a Choice

Every high school has a few shy girls, geeky girls, girls that don't quite fit into the cool crew. I was that shy girl in school, riddled with worry walking down to the bus stop because the school next door released their students five or ten minutes before my school. It meant that group of girls were coming for me.

Yes, I was bullied. I let their taunting and hair pulling affect me, hold me back, make me hide away and I became quite good at it.

It's not all doom and gloom. I am now a successful business owner. I have overcome confidence issues and torn my way through some difficult times, to come out of the other end, happy and enthusiastic about life and the opportunities it presents. I want to let you know that you can choose to be a more confident person: I did.

My confidence has always held me back until recently, but life experiences have really helped me find me. They have brought out the person who for so many years hid away. Through my experiences I have been able to connect with so many women on an emotional level and strive to help others through a unique form of therapy. This isn't counselling or the traditional methods which spring to mind when we hear the term 'therapy'.

Through the process and experience of makeup application I have seen women transform in confidence, their stress levels have been reduced and they feel empowered in various areas of their lives. This therapy works for both the therapist carrying out the treatment and also the person receiving the treatment.

I am going to share with you my ups and downs, to inspire you on your journey because our experiences shape us. I want to share with you how I used my life experiences to go on to help others and how in the process I also healed.

As a child, I wouldn't say I had many aspirational dreams growing up, particularly around the time I went to high school, I was too busy thinking up ways I could swerve the bullies after school. It's quite sad really, isn't it, how a few individuals can have such a big impact on your self-esteem and consequently damage your future.

My interests included running, horse riding, flicking through the pages of magazines and I always enjoyed applying makeup on myself. Tammy Girl was my favourite shop back in the 90s. I would buy eyeshadow palettes and roll on lip glosses.

It was like therapy – I felt good.

I remember around the age of fourteen going shopping with my mum every week and her saying to me, 'Don't tell your dad what we have bought and how much we have spent.' I loved our secret shopping trips. I had a good relationship with my parents, even if I told a few white lies to dad.

By the time I started college and finally got away from the dreaded bullies, I was starting to feel really good about myself and had an amazing couple of years making the most of all the opportunities I was given. My college course involved lots of teamwork and physical activity. I was a great team player, quite popular and had a great social life at this point. I started to think about my future and worked towards going to university. I'd be the second person in my whole family to go to university so I was excited to make the family proud.

My final year assessments started and then out of nowhere my mum left the family home, with no warning and no contact from her for some time.

I felt like my confidence was yet again back to ground zero. Stress and anxiety took over at what was a pivotal time in my life. I felt abandoned as both parents were absent from this moment. I wasn't a stranger to the feeling of anxiety. However, their vacant presence left me with such an empty feeling.

I was determined to go to uni, to be quite honest. I still had no idea what I wanted to do professionally and needed to buy some more time. I wished I had my career path all mapped out but I didn't have a mentor or anyone to support my decisions. This taught me a major lesson.

Don't feel discouraged. Everyone finds their own path in time. It's easy to envy others, especially when they look to have their shit together, but don't live your life on someone else's timeline.

I was working as a retail assistant, dipping my toe into admin from time to time. The responsibility of cashing up at the end of the day and the few years I had running my dad's furniture shop on a weekend made me play with the idea of studying retail management.

Towards the end of my three-year course, I was set on becoming a beauty buyer, travelling the world sourcing new ingredients, products, and networking with brands. None of this happened because I got married and very quickly was expecting my first baby. This change of direction taught me that life is so precious – don't just do what you think is expected of you in society, like graduating and going into an assistant role before moving your way up the ladder. Do what makes you feel happy and what feels right.

THE OUTSIDER, TRYING TO FIT IN.

I was living in my in-laws' house at this time. Of course, it was a new environment and I was feeling anxious. I felt those same emotions I had experienced before during other events in my life, such as the period of being bullied and when my parents divorced. This feeling never left me. I had this little human growing inside of me and it felt like a miracle that I was going to be a mum. I had so many ideas of how I wanted to raise my child, as I'm sure many of us do. I thought about the mistakes my parents had made and I was going to do better and be the perfect mum to my child.

At the age of 24, I had my first baby, Ayyaan. I had always had a strong passion to be a mum. In fact, when I say I never had any aspirations as a young girl, actually being a mum was always my desire. It's funny − I would imagine myself as one of those mums with a baby strapped to her back trekking through fields, up hills, doing the Great Wall of China and raising her baby around wild animals in Africa. I am a bit of a daydreamer.

So here I was living within a different culture to my own. My husband and his family are of Pakistani heritage and lived a very different lifestyle to my upbringing. Before marriage, I thought about the culture as being bright, fun, exciting, joyful, with big families and lots of love. Oh, it is!

I fitted in well. Everyone was supportive but over time I was starting to notice this anxious feeling was not going away. It was becoming worse. I describe walking down the stairs and into the living room every day as the nervous feeling you experience walking into an interview. Can you imagine having those kinds of nerves every day?

Having a baby within a large family has its pros and cons. My baby was very loved but as a new mum I felt he was being taken away from me. Things like bath-time were taken away from me, making decisions for him was taken away from me, and, of course, it was his big family all wanting to be a part of his life: how lucky was this little boy! But I was struggling! The overwhelm of having a large family around my brand-new baby and being pushed out, or so it felt, affected my mental health. This is something I have never admitted to until now.

Baby number two was on the way and I was determined to take back my control. The bitch in me wanted to burst out of my body at the slightest thought of anyone wanting to take over baby duties. Still living with my in-laws, my days consisted of cleaning, cooking, making my mother-in-law tea, and more of it.

It was expected of us to live within the family. The girls cooked and cleaned, and, well, my husband, he grafted. Each day was the same. I was starting to lose sight of myself; I couldn't remember who I was before. I rarely saw my friends and when I did they would comment on the way I was dressing and the way I spoke. They struggled to have any sort of conversation with me. Have you ever known someone to move to a different country and after some time, say two years, you notice their accent has changed, and they behave a little differently or dress a little differently because over time they have adjusted to their new life in that country? Well, that's the only way I can describe what was happening to me, living within a different culture to my own.

I felt cultural expectations upon me. I know some of you reading this will understand how I was feeling if you are in a cross-cultural relationship.

I could feel my character slipping away. I wasn't me; this (being at home, only cooking and cleaning) wasn't me. Heavily pregnant, with hormones flying around, I thought, it's now or never! I can do something for me or continue to fit in.

THE DECISION I WAS ABOUT TO MAKE WOULD CHANGE MY LIFE.

Heavily pregnant, I rocked up to an interview for an adult beauty therapy course at my local college. Head held high, crushing my nerves and not caring what others thought of my huge belly, I walked in there like it was the first day of the rest of my life.

I wasn't expecting the response I got from the course leaders. They thought it was too soon for me and suggested I try again the following year. But this was the first day of the rest of my life, right? Yes! I didn't take no for an answer. I begged and pleaded with them to give me a chance. This was my time to level up!

My second baby was three days old on my course start date. No excuses; I expressed my breastmilk and handed it to my husband. One evening a week for ME, to socialize and learn new skills. It was exactly what I needed.

It was on this evening course that I discovered my passion for makeup again. The other students would ask me for advice on applying makeup and I felt at ease showing them my techniques. This shy girl who lacked confidence was suddenly comfortable in an 'all eyes on me' group environment. At that very moment in that very class, I knew what I wanted to do as a career. Although it had probably been staring me right in the face, at the age of 26 I finally found the path I was destined for.

Oh, but that niggling confidence issue! It was still there but not so much of a problem because I was lucky enough to have friends who believed in me and a family who, despite my own insecurities in thinking I needed to fit into their box, supported me in anything I decided to do. I learned to be myself, not to try and always "fit in".

We moved out of the main family home and bought our 'first house'. I longed for this day, a day I never thought would come. Despite going against all the rules in the book it saved relationships with my in-laws and I wouldn't change that for anything.

Finally, everything was going great and I was ready to show up to the world. I started my business as a makeup artist – well, a social media account at least. It was a friend actually who set up a Facebook page for me. What are friends for? I still remember sitting on the edge of my bed with my first makeup picture ready to be published and saying to her, "Oh no, I don't think I can do it", "nobody will be interested", "I'm sure everyone will just have a good old laugh": AKA imposter syndrome. A lack of self-belief is in fact self-sabotage. Standing in your very own way is pernicious and can not only affect the decisions we make but the energy can have an impact on various aspects of our lives, from relationships to business and everything in between.

Not many makeup artists existed in my area then. Those that did only offered bridal or very natural makeup, so being the first one bringing a more glam style and putting it out there was daunting but something which was very much needed so I went for it. Unsurprisingly to everyone else, the response I got was amazing. These positive reactions made me realise that there are many more people out there wanting to see you succeed than there are who want to see you fail. At this point, I was focused on getting one or two bookings per week but I had more inquiries than I had anticipated. It took off!

I was travelling out to clients, visiting them in their homes, meeting their families, friends and neighbours, and word spread about my services. My confidence grew in many ways; people liked my work and trusted me to get them ready for special events. Just being out of the home, meeting new people, having social interactions is what was missing when I was a stay at home mum and wife.

Speaking with other women I soon realised I wasn't alone in the way I was feeling, that lost feeling when you're no longer who you once were and the craving to be more than a woman who should be tied to the kitchen sink.

ASPIRATIONS WERE FORMED.

I was a mum of two boys and in a great place in my life. I was able to be at home with them throughout the week, spending real quality time with them. When I was with my boys I was fully with them because I was happy! *It was my well-being boosting activity; makeup.* When you're happy those around you are too. Who doesn't want their family to be happy? I encourage everyone to make their own happiness a priority.

As my business grew, I built up a regular client base and decided that travelling out to their homes wasn't something I wanted to do any longer. I started to develop a business brain and worked out that if they came to me it would save me x amount of time, I could fit more clients in and make more money.

My home salon was born. When I say salon, I mean my dining room. I had everything set up perfectly and my appointments ran smoothly. Bringing clients into my home, especially the regular ones, meant that better relationships formed. They would stay and cuddle my cat and speak to my children. It's a known fact that people buy from people, so I think this decision really helped further my business.

Working from home was great for a little while. It meant I wasn't stuck in traffic on a Saturday afternoon; however, it also meant the home had to be pristine, the children well-presented and I had to have a firm word with my husband and children before each client to ensure not too much noise and strictly no arguing or fighting. Oh yes, it happened a lot!

I became so busy that maintaining a professional-ish environment was becoming more difficult. My children wanted their home back. They didn't want to have to be quiet any longer. We had baby number three on the way, and that professional environment I was trying to maintain was slipping further and further out of my hands. Since starting my business I always pictured having my very own makeup studio. I even designed it in my mind and would create Pinterest boards full of ideas. There goes my imagination running wild again.

IT HAPPENED!

After many months of searching, I found my dream shop, and *Laura Nazir Makeup Studio* popped up on the high-street. I had big plans. It wasn't just about me anymore. I wanted to make a difference to other people. I thought about the feeling I got when I finished each and every client's makeup. It was this overwhelming, warm sensation at the smile on their face as they saw their makeup complete. My services made them feel good and instantly their confidence skyrocketed; the way they would hold themselves and the way they would look at themselves in the mirror was so rewarding for me.

So, I wanted to create a professional space that would make my clients feel comfortable, relaxed, and give them an enjoyable experience, from the moment they walked in. *Makeup should be an experience: it is therapy after-all.* For me, it's always been about how something can make you feel from the inside out. You can walk in with the weight of the world on your shoulders and walk out ready to take on anything, if that isn't therapy then I don't know what is. As a makeup artist, it feels so powerful to be able to make this small but significant change to someone's day or mood.

I had started to build a good reputation in my area for the services I provided. Girls would often comment on the shop. I wanted a really clean feeling, not too clinical but a space which felt light, bright, and airy. It was certainly a hit. They would tell me how well I had done and congratulate me on my success. It made me feel really good and proud of how far I had come from only being mum, wife, and daughter-in-law. Don't get me wrong, I feel so blessed to have each and every one of them around me and to be someone they need. However, I couldn't help but reminisce about my journey which got me to that point. I had some really low moments, and I didn't ever want to go back there and then it occurred to me that I hadn't experienced the anxiety I had previously for quite some time. Now that was an achievement. *It is important to look back every now and then, only to see how far you have come.*

SELF-BELIEF IS A POWERFUL THING.

Fast forward a year or so and I still felt like there was so much more I could give in terms of helping other women.

In 2019 I trained to be a therapy lecturer. I wanted to reach women who, like me, needed a creative output, something to take them from mummy to 'me' for a few hours each week. I opened up an opportunity for women in the area to easily access education and gain a qualification which would allow them entry into the professional beauty world. I partnered with a professional trade body to provide both online and in-person training. I officially had a registered school for adult learning.

In my seven years as a professional makeup artist, working alongside other creatives and professionals in the industry, I had picked up a wealth of knowledge and practical skills which I knew would benefit women wanting to start up their own businesses. Being asked on countless occasions how I started and how I had managed to open my own studio specialising in makeup, made me completely sure that others would want to learn from me and I really believed I had the capability of helping, training, and mentoring women who wanted to do exactly what I had done.

YOU ARE ENOUGH.

My goal was to enrol women onto a group course with my main focus on teaching various styles of makeup because I thought this was something I had to do as an academy, "an industry-standard" although a bright colourful cut-crease wasn't really "my style". After some time not really loving what I was creating, it occurred to me that my students booked me as their trainer for a reason and the reason was that they were drawn to my style. I put ME into every look I taught and it absolutely paid off. The course was successful, my students enjoyed their practical sessions and so did I. I was delighted with their response to the course, although the structure wasn't quite right, but a little tweaking and I had mastered it. My new students were incredible; their practical skills blew me away. *Be yourself, always!*

Month on month, I was running the four-week accredited makeup training course with success or so I thought.

Many of my students went on to start up their own businesses; however, many also didn't. I wanted to know why that was. They had all the practical and theoretical knowledge they needed to be able to deliver makeup services to a high standard. Surely they should be taking bookings.

After some digging, I pieced together all the feedback I acquired. It was insightful, a real turning point for me to up-level again. I found out that from the students I had taught, that the women who desired to start their own business as a professional makeup artist in the beauty industry post-qualification did not do so due to CONFIDENCE.

I had to do something about this.

I saw a way to improve and add dimension to my courses, have more impact on these women, and empower them and that's exactly what I do now.

I have developed my courses with women at their heart. I have found out exactly what it is they need from me, the person who has struggled with a lack of self-confidence yet still managed to push through and build a successful business. I have done all the groundwork and used trial and error so that I can help others. One thing I possibly would have done a little sooner in hindsight and would recommend anyone to do is, *invest in yourself.* I would have saved myself so much time and money if I had worked with a coach or mentor.

The advice I would give to any woman wanting to start a career in the beauty industry is: work hard and have determination, because being a female founder isn't easy but it is one of the most rewarding things you will do.

I am now considered an expert hair and makeup educator, beauty business mentor, and empowerment *coach.*

I work with women I connect with and women who want to make a change in their lives. I am a performance-driven trainer who delivers practical courses, with outstanding results both in my learners' practical skills and drive. They have confidence in their capabilities and determination to succeed, equipped with the know-how to do it. I am my learners' biggest supporter because I believe in them and I believe in myself.

Mindset plays a huge part in your successes. Trust that your life experiences will shape you, know that you have choices, and be sure to reach up high and grab what is meant for you. Be unstoppable!

I want women from all backgrounds and professions to put their happiness first, get up every day, and live their best life with a positive mindset. I want women who have struggled and those who are currently struggling with the various curve balls which life throws at us, to find their unique form of therapy, that thing which makes you glow from within, that thing which helps your mind see everything else much clearer.

I will never stop learning and growing but I will always continue to do what I am passionate about, put my happiness first, and empower other women to do the same. I'm so excited for what is to come: please hop on my train and ride this journey with me — next stop, worldwide online training and mentoring. I will reach women who need me wherever they are in the world.

Thank-you to each and every person who has brought something to my life.

Laura Nazir.

ABOUT THE AUTHOR

Laura Nazir

Laura Nazir is a heart-centered therapy lecturer who helps women fulfil their ambition of turning their passion for makeup into a successful business with the inclusion of business coaching.

Sharing the exact formula she used to establish Laura Nazir Makeup Studio in 2017. Laura also helps existing artists upscale their business to include or specialise in luxury bridal through her 'level up' course.

Her passion and enthusiasm to empower women and, to help build their confidence are felt by many, from her fellow industry connections to her audience and clientele.

She has been put forward for industry awards year on year by members of the public who respect her as an artist and educator. She has also been published in the guild gazette trade magazine, as a school to watch.

Laura is a busy mum to three children, she created a home-life, work-life balance, to take her from stay at home mum and wife to someone who felt empowered, well-rounded, and happy in life.

Her mission is to help and inspire other women to find there's too and to introduce them to the wonderful industry of makeup, business, and beyond.

CONTACT:

Email address:
info@lauranazirmakeupstudio.co.uk
Website:
www.lauranazirmakeupstudio.co.uk

facebook.com/hairandmakeupeducation
instagram.com/laura_nazir_makeup_studio

14

NATASHA GULLIFORD

Don't Let Road blocks Determine Your Destination

THE BEGINNING

During a recent conversation with one of my one to one clients I realised I had become a millionaire.

I'm not bathing in £50 notes just yet. But I have reached that point in my life where I can look around and feel 'rich' in my environment. I have built a life I love, and now I'm helping others to do so as well.

I am someone who is very much guided by the things I have learnt and have been advised. As a visual person, I always have my eyes and ears open ready to absorb my surroundings. It is often just a passing comment, or an almost insignificant thing that has crossed my path, which had the power to determine it. As I look back, these have been the signposts that have navigated me through my career, some for better, and some for worse.

My story starts with a casual remark from my University tutor. Although inconsequential to some, I saw it in neon lights because it made everything click into place.

'If you want a job in the textiles industry, learn to paint flowers.'

You see, there were parts during my textiles degree that made me second guess my career choice. I've always been an artist to my core, but the knowledge of fast fashion, the beginnings of the digital era, and the realisation that there were hundreds of us, so what would make me different, why would anyone choose me, had greyed my bright future. But this bridged the gap between digital and hand-done, between art and fashion; it was me in my happy place... but commercially! From this, I managed to get a design job before I even graduated from University. I loved it and felt like I had hit the jackpot.

I paint flowers. Okay, maybe a bit more than that. What I really do is design floral patterns that are printed onto various products across multiple industries worldwide, from fashion to homeware, stationery and beyond. Hey, you might even own something of mine.

This advice was one of those serendipitous moments, the advice I am forever grateful for taking. But advice hasn't always been this advantageous.

One that moulded me for some time is a conversation I had with a colleague during my first years in the design industry. She told me, *"You don't get into the textiles industry to make millions."*

My inexperienced naivety took those words as gospel and it put a real damper on my youthful enthusiasm to drive forward in my career. For a while I let it determine my life and limit my aspirations and because of this, I was left just going through the motions; creating a treadmill of SSDD (same sh*t, different day).

Now don't get me wrong, it was all the good type of sh*t. I was working for one of the largest print design studios in London which I loved, had great bosses, and a great network of colleagues who soon became friends. My week consisted of pub lunches, Thursday cocktails, and Friday afternoon 'design raves'. But with the good also came the bad. These were long expensive commutes, a small, over-priced rental, and a feeling that this work/life model was unbalanced – an inkling of being overworked and underpaid.

For a while, I couldn't see any other way than working my 9-5, as my ambitions were clouded by those negative words. Since then I have thankfully been able to ignore such pessimistic thrown around remarks as I have risen to be a glass half-full kind'a gal. But back then I let it control my work which subsequently meant it controlled my income and therefore life was a strain as we struggled to pay the bills and try to enjoy living the lifestyle we wanted to. We were living month to month on a maxed-out overdraft having recurring nightmares of that final demand notice.

The next few years of my career were much the same; I enjoyed it, and I made a good living out of it, but I wasn't feeling fulfilled and it was during that time that my then-boyfriend, now husband, got offered a job outside of London. Being a Somerset girl who left the countryside for the big city lights I was in two minds about moving back, but I took the leap of faith as I thought it could be the change I needed to be inspired again.

Boy, was I right, as I welcomed my new life as a freelancer.

THE HUSTLE

Freelancing isn't for everyone. As you can imagine, it takes a lot of self-discipline, quite a bit of hustling, and a ton of creativity. BUT I LOVED IT. I was on fire.

I continued to work with the same studio on a freelancer/agent basis, to maintain a great relationship with them and solidify my customer base. But I soon realised that the opportunities as a freelancer were endless.

The dial was turned up a notch because I was my own art director. I was designing things I would never have designed in-house. Creativity was oozing out of me; I had ideas galore. I pushed myself in different directions and my sales were reflective of this. As an in-house designer, I felt a little pigeon-holed, but I understood the reasons for it. I was playing my part in a successful and diverse collection which required no repetition to keep it fresh and new.

But to then be in a position to break that mould was revolutionising for me. Alongside this, which had become my 'bread and butter' income, I had also managed to get some regular commissioned client work with indie brands helping design their collections, and even landed some high-end designers too. All of this resulted in a lucrative design business all from painting flowers.

But this is not how I became a millionaire.

I had managed to buy my own house, yes, whilst also finding the balance between countryside and city living, perching myself on the south side of Bristol. But for me it wasn't the money that lit the fire in my belly, it was the freedom of creation. I had finally ditched the SSDD treadmill lifestyle and my days now consisted of researching, mood boarding, trend analysing, painting, designing, audiobook listening as well as conversing, pitching and pursuing new clients… where I could see a collaboration would benefit the both of us. Through my social media, I was also getting clients coming to me too. It was exciting and rewarding, but what I loved more was the freedom of working when I wanted and where I wanted. Whether that was painting on the beach in Mexico, or on the canyons in LA, I had finally found a great work/life balance.

Now, I don't want to paint this glossy picture like I had this perfect life. I worked hard and often worked weekends to meet deadlines. As well as all the design stuff, I was also the accountant, admin, and customer services; I was wearing all the hats. And I'm not going to pretend I was selling fifty designs every month either. This is the design industry, and with all design there are trends that come and go, and sometimes... you're just not that fashionable.

This is when it's time to switch it up: more research, more testing, and more hard work! If you don't you will get stuck spiralling down the rabbit hole of doing the same stuff that isn't working. Business is ever-growing, ever-developing and ever-changing. You need to be prepared to change with it.

For me, the hardest part of being a Solopreneur is the loneliness. If you ever spend five minutes in my company, virtually or face to face, you will soon realise I'm pretty chatty. I thrive off of personal connection and come alive making new relationships. This is one thing that I loved from my first job. That buzz of creativity chatting shop with your colleagues, mixed with a bit of daily gossip or our thoughts on last night's episode of 'The Fall' (this was 2013). But now my work life had become all the cake and no topping, and we all need a little chocolate ganache in our lives.

Whilst I was loving what I did, that niggle of un-fulfilment came creeping back in and this is where an idea was born.

In 2018 I created a Facebook group called 'Let's Paint Flowers'. The idea was to create a virtual studio environment to connect with other designers, artists, and creatives aspiring to be so. I wanted to create a safe space for people to ask questions and share work. Once up and running, it was filling that gap I was craving, the social connection and the creative community, but what I was also doing was helping people.

With it came a load of people wanting mentoring and a little guidance on how to get into the industry. As they became more regular, I even mentored a few on a one to one basis to help them build portfolios that got them jobs and their first design gigs. I found a passion that I hadn't even planned. Starting this group was to be the beginning of something, I just didn't know what yet. I was taking a couple of courses to learn the ins and outs of business, and all the behind-the-scenes tech that it involved (I learned that there is a lot). It was a fantastic year for me all round as my personal life was moving at the same pace. I got married in the May and soon afterwards I fell pregnant.

THE FIGHT

We all know childbirth is hard, right, but what people do not talk enough about, is how hard it is afterwards. Following a very un-planned birth, and a traumatic set of events after that, being failed by a system we put our lives in the hands of, I had lost all confidence and the ability to trust in the expected. I was left feeling a shell of the person I once was.

As a chatty extrovert, I've always been very good at hiding the inner demon of self-belief. As a sleep-deprived mother recovering from surgery and fighting to get the care I needed to get well, I allowed the demon to win the battle as I let the extrovert lay down in that dark place. This is where I turned to art. I've always been an artist to my core, and in an attempt to claw myself into the light I started to paint again. I was flooded with comments of, *"You should be sleeping,"* and, *"I can't believe you're working already,"* people not knowing the battle I was facing internally as I replied with a brave face and a funny comment.

This was both the hardest and most rewarding time in my life. I had an angel in my arms but it didn't feel like heaven. So every time I put her down for a nap I would pick up my paintbrush and start painting, and with every brushstroke, I would find a little piece of me again. It's true what they say, art really is a healer. Meditate, paint, create: the peaceful practise of painting allowed me time to think, adjust and finally take deep breaths. It was like I was seeing myself in third person. ME the carefree designer watching ME 'the lost mum'. But as I painted, I began to become one again because it allowed me to JUST BE ME for a second. Although I had become a new version of myself, the old me still existed in there somewhere, I just needed to find her. When we become mothers, we put all of our needs and wants to one side and would draw blood from a stone to provide for our children. It's so important to remember that these minis need their mamas well. Feed the body, feed the mind and feed the soul. Whatever change has come into your life and flipped it upside down or torn you apart, allow yourself some YOU time so you can become whole again.

Needless to say, during this time, the Facebook group had been left alone and had become dormant. It felt like all my hard work had been wasted and what was developing into a new beginning seemed like mountains to climb to get everything back to where it once was.

THE COVID COMEBACK

This brings me to more current affairs and to the pandemic we are currently living in, Covid-19. Just as I was designing at full steam again the world went into lockdown. For a minute I thought of giving up. Maybe I'll just be a stay at home mum, at least that was predictable (ish). But however much I loved my girl to the end of the earth and went to bed looking forward to our morning cuddles, I needed something for me too.

Covid hit hard. I was owed thousands of pounds in unpaid sales due to the closure of retail shops worldwide. But once I had emerged from that realisation, I was able to see the bigger picture. What was prominent to me was the number of people who were potentially alone and struggling. Not just artists, but home workers, designers out of work, the furloughed, the retired and grandparents, etc. Loneliness is a silent killer. I felt it as a freelancer and I felt it as a new mother confined to the home as I healed from surgery. The world was gambling with the unknown and who knew how long it would last?

I took this as a sign and an opportunity to pick up where I left off with my online community. I was one of those designers out of work so knew that there would be a lot of people struggling too. I jumped in headfirst, without a plan (which is very unlike me). You see, I'm very much an 'I need all the facts and figures' kind'a girl. But the time was now because people needed this, so there was no time to overthink.

I'm very much your typical artist. I'm very good with the practical, but me and tech aren't always friends. Along with that self-belief monster who sits on my shoulder and nibbles my ear from time to time (not in a sexy way), they have been excuses that have stopped me in my tracks during the many times I've started new ventures before.

I've always learned from the best to try and be the best, but I've never put myself on that podium and worn the label of 'expert'. Although I knew I had the knowledge, the experience, and a willingness to share, the thought of putting myself out there with that label was scary. I felt vulnerable and it made me uncomfortable. Sitting still with a heavy weight of imposter syndrome on my shoulders I went around in circles asking myself, *who was I to teach? How will I translate everything in a digestible way? Will I even be able to help others?*

With the support of my husband who told me I just needed to do it, in slightly stronger words, I brushed off my demons and I put my passion out into the world of social media; I'm teaching a free painting bootcamp, come and get it! With no idea how I was actually going to present said course, I started planning it. There is a lot of love for watercolours, and I figured it was something that people might have in their craft box. I wanted it to be inclusive, help all levels, and allow everybody to be able to learn from it. At this point, I intended to create that community feel. To bring back that safe space for people to share work, to give others something fun and light-hearted and to provide focus whilst the world was up in the air.

Through sharing and engaging my art, I had designed a space where painting could be the saviour for others like it had been once for me.

It's never just simple though is it? Here came another lot of research, but not the pretty mood board type; this time, the dreaded tech! Cameras, lighting, tripods and programmes, things that would have normally been another roadblock and would have made me veer left, but instead I put the pedal to the metal and the six-week Watercolour Bootcamp came to life.

Its purpose was the community, a creative place to create a constant whist the world was in chaos. One week in and it was already thriving with positivity. The diversity of levels was vast, and it brought in a range of people. Mothers were painting with their daughters for home-schooled art classes, the furloughed were picking up a new hobby, and designers who had been designing since before I was born were able to learn the art of florals and add another string to their bow. Each taking part, equally as supportive and together spurring along their peers.

This was a massive leap for me, and I had never felt so fulfilled in my career. This was making a difference to people. I was buzzing; this was exactly what I wanted to do, to allow people to do something they love, something they're excited about, and be the person to help them achieve it. It was an incredible feeling.

What was more astonishing than ever was the improvement I saw as the creatives shared their paintings throughout the six weeks. What had started as a simple creative community, had become a lively class of water-colour artists. This was the validation that I needed.

I do have knowledge worth sharing.

I can translate what I know into bitesize pieces.

I can help people do what they love.

And what's more, what they were asking is… *"what's next?"*

The funny thing with success is that once you get a bit of it, whether that's good grades, a winning trophy, a good first date, selling some work or bagging a great client, and in my case, creating a course that people were loving, it both fires you up and makes you second guess your next steps. I guess that's the protector in us. The part of our brain that doesn't want us to get hurt, and although it might be keeping us out of harm's way, it is also getting in the damn way! The questions of *'what do you have planned next'* were being fired my way.

'Next?' I thought. 'I'm only just catching my breath.'

True to one of my most lived by mantras, 'If it's not broken don't fix it,' I acted in the same way I would when seeing successful trends as a designer; I continued along the path that was in demand. I needed to create some-thing new and fresh, something that was going to answer a lot of people's problems. I wrote things down that I knew and could convert into teachings and well… I needed a bigger piece of paper!

Although I had hungry customers and tons of knowledge to share, I could see so many hurdles between this page full of ideas and physically being able to create a course to sell. I had no website, no copy, no form of taking payments, no brand photography (this was lockdown so no options for a photoshoot either). I was looking after my daughter full time and working 8pm - 2am to get it all done. I booked coaching sessions to make sure I was on the right track, and to have someone keep me account-able. I knew my track record for things like this. I would historically come to a stop!

It was a crazy two months and whilst everyone was making tiktoks, day drinking, and suddenly becoming Alan Titchmarsh, I was building a new business.

If you've ever put yourself out there and asked someone to invest in you, I'm sure you've shared these feelings. Whether it's a job interview, asked someone to critique a portfolio, created a product, sent a quote, or designed a workshop, you have those inner feelings of self-doubt.

I had poured my entire ten years into a course covering something everyone was asking for, but still at the forefront of my mind was… *'Will anyone buy it… please, please let someone buy it.'*

I priced it low; this was a beta run.

At first, I thought, *'If no one buys it, it's fine, it was worth a try.'*

As I re-read the content my confidence grew to, '*If five people buy it, I'll be happy.*'

It was launch week.

I sold 35 spaces in the first 48 hours, totalling 41 by cart closed! Picking my jaw up off the floor, I happy danced around the kitchen so thankful I had the confidence FINALLY, to just do it!

My 'students', who all consisted of professional designers and artists, were raring to go. The course became more than I had ever expected and from week one, they were already selling their designs. I had messages from them with their sales updates, commission enquiries, and comments of '*Module 3... game changer*', and that it was '*the best thing that happened to me in 2020*'. I let out that sigh of relief. I had created a course that was making a difference and helping people achieve their goals to create a life they love, just like I did. Alongside this was a community of 41 professional creatives who were all from different backgrounds, all sharing their industry knowledge, as I was sharing mine too.

For me, the success of the course isn't how many places I sold, it's how many lives it has changed. With the textile industry, you are the tin of beans without the label. We create countless artworks and designs for other brands to put their name to, which I've always been fine with because I love what I do. But this felt like receiving that winning trophy with my name engraved on it. The credibility that I'm good at what I do.

If this journey has taught me anything, it's to ride the wave even if you're not that great a swimmer. I've heard every excuse in the book because it's possible that I wrote the book. When I think back to the person I was just trying to stay afloat and find that creative spark inside me again, it seems like a decade ago. Yet in just two months I created a business I had wanted to do for years, and it took a catastrophe to do it. In years to come, when I look back to the pandemic of 2020, I will remember the lives lost of course, and the heroes in blue that saved so many lives, but I will also remember the world giving me a virtual slap and pushing me into my next level. If you're resonating with anything you've read here... don't wait until the next pandemic to start your venture, do it now!

So as I was saying, I was having a conversation with my one to one client and we reflected on our lives so far as textiles designers; our luck of being able to do a career we love, and the ability to call flower painting 'work'. We were diving deep into how success is different for all of us. For me, I'm not in it for the money, I'm in it for the love of what I do, both design and now teaching. I laughed as I told her that flippant comment from my colleague all those years ago, and confirmed, I didn't want to be a millionaire. But as we sat talking biz, she gave me a little teaching too... and that's when I realised...

I have built a life I love. I have a home, a loving family who are my everything, and a successful lucrative business which I look forward to clocking on to every single day. I get to create art and chat with other creatives about art, design and fashion… and call it 'work'.

What more could I want? I am a millionaire.

I guess what I'm trying to say is that if you have a dream, make it a goal.

Put your grown-up shoes on and strut your way through those hurdles. Pack away your protective jacket for a second and put on your tool belt and overalls. Things are going to be a little hard, they're going to be a little messy, but a lot can come from owning the knowledge you have.

Sometimes it takes that little wobble, that knockdown that takes your breath away and is hard to sit up from to make you realise how much you can take. I can take some light with me from those darker days as they built a stronger woman, one that marched across those bumpy roads, climbed those tall mountains, and ultimately has ended up on top of the world.

Oh, and whilst we're on that note: it is most definitely VERY possible to make seven figures as a textiles designer, but that's a topic for another day.

ABOUT THE AUTHOR

Natasha Gulliford

Natasha Gulliford is an international textiles designer, who designs for a variety of industries from fashion, home-wares and various other products. As a successful designer her work has been featured in the collections of many established and well-known brands like Anthropology, Project D, ASOS, Phase Eight, Oasis and Paperchase, to name a few. Natasha specialises in hand painted floral artwork to which she has built an extensive client base for her signature style.

As a multifaceted designer and artist, she is also an educator and mentor, teaching a worldwide audience the art of florals and their power in design. She has guided many of her students to create consumer driven designs enabling them to be 'featured designers' on large pattern design platforms.

Natasha is a community leader who thrives off the power of connection, collaboration and is an advocate of supporting and helping others to rise. As a passionate educator she is dedicated to sharing her decade of industry knowledge to other creatives to aid them in their creative journey.

Her mission is to help others to create a life they love by using their creative business as the instrument to do so.

CONTACT:

Email:
natasha@natashagulliford.com
Website:
www.natashagulliford.com

Let's Paint Flowers Facebook Group:
www.facebook.com/groups/letspaintflowers

facebook.com/iamnatashagulliford
instagram.com/natasha.gulliford

15

NIKI FRENCH

I. Am. Inevitable.

WHY DIDN'T I JUST TELL SOMEONE?

I have a really crap memory. I mean like goldfish crap. I can watch a film and then re-watch it a year later and be at least halfway through it before I realise, hang on, I've seen it before (facepalm).

It does mean that recalling events and details from my life can be tricky. Some people seem to be able to remember so much from when they were young. For me, there are massive gaps punctuated with some hazy memories and the odd thing that I remember so clearly, it's like I've just watched a scene from a film. But mostly I have to work hard to dig memories out. Or randomly remember something bizarre while chatting over a glass of wine.

There's one childhood memory that is too easy to recall. I'm in the toilets of my school gym, three cubicles on the left, 'run through' showers on the right (we were all so shy of showing our bodies at that age we'd just drop our towels and run through as quickly as possible to get wet and then scurry to get covered up again). This very tall girl has me in a head lock and she's dragging me towards the middle toilet bowl, while two smaller mean-faced girls laugh and taunt me. She's trying to flush my head down the toilet.

I even remember her full name, and there are very few names I remember from school without looking at my carefully labelled school photos.

There's a scuffle and I break free and I run off and, for the first time, finally tell the games teacher all about it.

This was the peak of me being bullied for a couple of years. Until this point, I hadn't told anyone. I was far too scared to. And miraculously, it just stopped. All the fear, all the tears, all the stress, all the upset. The power these bullies had over me was incredible. I looked backed for years afterwards thinking, why didn't I tell someone sooner? At the time, there didn't even remotely seem to be anything I could do.

But being bullied did teach me something. No matter how helpless a situation feels, there is always something that we can do. The choices we make, the actions we take, even just how we think about things, there is always something that is within our control.

It also started building the foundations of something else. The older I get, the more I realise how resilient I am. No matter what was going on at school I kept on going and kept on studying hard. Even as an adult, and days were tough going at work, I would still keep on going. Even if I had to go and have a bit of a cry before getting stuck back into whatever was causing me stress. I don't get derailed for long.

I remember being a really outgoing kid. We used to go camping many weekends of the year and this meant meeting and making new 'best friends' wherever we were that weekend. I'd happily to chat to any new kids my sister and I would meet, and we'd be making up games in minutes. I've many happy memories of our own 'one-man' tents pitched outside our parents' trailer tent. We called them pup tents for some reason. And we'd be cooking some strange, dehydrated soup on a single gas stove. I'm old enough to remember the seemingly never-ending heat wave summer of '76. Shining swarms of lady-birds, metres deep at the edges of the sea. I collected a few in a clear box with some leaves in it. I wanted to take some home as pets.

But I found school tough going. Not because of the work. I wasn't the brightest, but I worked hard. I never really had a solid group of girlfriends. I never felt like I really fitted in. I had one best friend, Victoria, who didn't really fit in either. Together we were a giggling team. We'd have fits of uncontrollable giggles; so bad we'd not be allowed to sit next to each other in class.

But other than Victoria, I didn't fit in. I didn't have a network of close friends I talked to when I was scared. I felt very alone a lot of the time. Sometimes I was ill – probably induced by stress. Sometimes I'd pretend to be ill so that I didn't have to go to school. This didn't work often enough, although I did go into hospital twice for suspected appendicitis. It's no surprise to me that I still have my appendix!

The head flushing in the toilet cubicle scuffle was the height (or depth?), and thankfully, the end of the bullying that had been festering for years.

It cemented a long-held belief in me that some girls are just mean.

I became quite distant from girls and didn't have many close girlfriends until very recently. This continued for most of my adult life. Conversely, I felt completely comfortable in the company of men. This became very useful in later life as I worked in male-dominated environments.

WHO ARE YOU CALLING FAT?

As part of the bullying I got called fat. Bullies are so unimaginative! I look at photos now and I wasn't fat but compared to my very slender sister and slender friends, I always felt bigger. I was an easy target. This is still a battle for me today. Like a lot of people, I turned to food to comfort myself. My body image is still not good, and I enviously watch ample woman walking confidently around in bikinis on holiday. I love it when people obviously love their bodies, whatever shape, or size. I have one, it works, and I want to embrace that.

This was the start of four decades of battling with my weight. But it's about more than what I weigh; it's about struggling to love myself, no matter what I look like. I was rejected by the bullying girls, and I didn't get support from the friends around me. I don't think I told them much about it, to be fair. But it felt like they were just glad it wasn't them being picked on and they didn't want to get involved. It all added to the feelings of rejection and not being good enough.

My body is relatively fit and well and I have so much to be grateful for. I get very cross with myself for not being able to just love me as I am. But I do now love the part of me that is incredibly brave. To have achieved so much in my first 51 years. To have had a high-level boardroom career for over two decades. To leave behind one successful career and start all over again doing something completely different. To leave a marriage that was making me so unhappy. To open myself up to believing everything is possible if I truly want it and work towards it. And working with dogs full time is that passion. It might have taken thirty years for me to reconnect with my childhood dream, but I'm doing it now.

BUT IT GAVE ME SKILLS

The bullying made me want to disappear into the background. Far better to be ignored than picked on – right? But, although it made me freak out in front of any kind of audience for ALL of my adult life, it gave me a really useful skill. I can be a real chameleon in any group of people; in my old life, whatever the meeting needed from me to be the most productive, I could take on that role. If the meeting needed to be taken control of, I would chair and get things moving. If things were getting fractious and people were getting heated with each other, I could see the common ground between people and bring them together with the areas they agreed on. If people were just talking for the sake of it, and we were running over time, I could bring it tactfully to a close. This skill served me so well over the years – the skill of adaptability, no matter what my natural personality type, to suit what needs to happen around me.

So, I had a career where I was on the rise, getting regular promotions every few years. This meant I was quickly in a position of managing a team of people of all ages when I was still in my twenties. I had an incredibly supportive Managing Director (thank you, Stuart!) who saw potential in me. And with each opportunity he gave me I was terrified, EVERY time, that I wouldn't be up to the new role. But it always seemed to work out ok.

Some people seem to get worried when they're approaching thirty, but I remember being really glad to be thirty as I thought it would help people take me 'more seriously'. It's not that they didn't, but in my head, I had a hang up that I needed the credibility of age rather than just what I was capable of. Ah, those nagging insecurities – please accept me, please like me!

BRING ON THE SPOTLIGHT

Despite struggles with my body image, my fierce desire to bring my games-based dog training to as many people as possible has forced me to make videos where there is no hiding my curvy shape. I can't just do head and shoulder videos and social media 'lives'. There is no choice but to bend over and point my butt towards the camera at times! I keep focused on the fact that people are watching the dog and what I'm doing with the dog. I don't judge other people physically, so why would other people judge me?

Mostly they probably don't. And if they do, why should their opinion matter to me? If they do, they're not 'my kind of people' and don't matter (the more I say this, the more I believe it).

In the words of Oscar Wilde, "Be yourself, everyone else is taken."

I also used to really dislike the sound of my voice. I thought I sounded posh and I've always had a hang-up about people thinking I'm posh. I think it was part of the nasty comments that were thrown at me by the bullies. It was only a local comprehensive school but compared to them I guess I seemed posh. To this day, I'm always quick to tell people I was born in Keighley, Yorkshire, as if that will help people like me when they hear my well-spoken voice!

I made myself a lockdown goal of starting a podcast. I want to spread current dog-training knowledge, in easy to listen to episodes, out to as many people as possible and this is a great way to do it. So I started a podcast. And there is absolutely no avoiding your own voice when you're editing and promoting your own podcast each week! It's actually been great therapy! My voice is now just that. My voice. And I have one. And I'm no longer afraid to use it.

I had a crippling fear of presenting, of anything that involved standing up in front of people, of being the centre of attention. I had it on my wedding day, with every kind of presentation, at every board meeting, staff update meeting, and team briefing. It was always there, the nagging doubt that I would forget what I needed to say. It taught me to get well prepared; if I was well prepared and had some sensible notes, I could get through it.

I still get nervous about being the centre of attention. I used to freak out at the thought of hitting the live button on Facebook – what would I say? But I did it anyway. Yes, I'm still scared about putting myself in front of any kind of audience. But I have too much I want to do to let it stop me. Plus, I find it infinitely easier if I have a dog by my side!

Most people had no idea how nervous I was. Everyone thought I was very confident and in control at work. Ah, little did they know! It made me work very hard; I felt I had to. But I felt that being able to work so hard was something to be proud of.

JUST BECAUSE YOU CAN, DOESN'T MEAN YOU SHOULD KEEP GOING

My sister is very bright, and although I wasn't stupid, I had to work very hard at school to get half decent grades. I definitely didn't feel smart enough or good enough. I was average. But it also gave me a sense that if I worked really hard at something, I could do OK. I was good at artistic subjects and it taught me to appreciate what I am good at and use that.

I had a part-time job at Sainsbury's supermarket while I was at Art College. All good training for the crumpled bar codes we now deal with at the self-service checkouts. I discovered I had a massive capacity to work really hard. I like earning my own money; I loved the feeling of control over my life and what I could afford.

I also didn't know how to slow down and listen to my body. I was ill with colds, throat infections and, eventually, kidney infections from working too many hours on top of studying. I used to wear hard work like a badge of honour; I was proud of how I could keep going if I had to. This 'skill' was very useful over the next thirty years of corporate life. It's not one I'd recommend though.

Working for myself, it's made me much more aware of the importance of being sustainable with the energy I expend. As a solopreneur, the plate spinning needed can leave my head spinning. But I want to carry on enjoying my new career, the new life I've worked so hard to create. I've built a life I don't want to retire from. And if I get ill, everything stops. And there are so many more people that I want to reach!

I dropped out of Art College after three years; I realised that I was distinctly average, and the fashion industry was not the place to be average. I thought I might as well just start earning some money.

Financial security is something I've always valued so highly, from my first job gardening in a care home, and cleaning horse brasses for extra pocket money at home. I think fifty pence a week was the going rate then. Going through an expensive divorce, selling my two buy-to-let flats and having a new mortgage at the age of 48 was very hard for me. I had the luxury of savings in the bank to live off while I got a new career and my own business off the ground, but I had to work hard to keep the financial security gremlins in my head at bay.

I spent time working on my money mindset; I didn't know I had one 18 months ago. Have you thought about yours? Useful questions I asked myself included thinking about how I was raised to view money; what my parents taught me about money; what limiting beliefs did I have about money? I even wrote out some affirmations to look at daily to help flip the switch of negative thought patterns about money and my new business. I'm not a very 'woo' person but I could see I needed to change my thinking.

I'm definitely still a workaholic; I'm not good at putting my mental and physical health first. When I worked for someone else I felt the pressure, the need to do it. But now I'm my own boss, I still do it! The problem is, what I'm doing now doesn't feel like work. It's too easy just too keep going. There's so much I want to achieve, so many people I want to reach, I can't get there fast enough.

FINDING BALANCE AND ACCEPTING THE UNKNOWN

I can't remember the last time I had balance in my life. It's so easy for me to fall into work; work is easy. It can be hard and gruelling and stressful and upsetting. But it can also be invigorating and fun and light me up. But it's like a drug that I find too addictive. I'm still learning how to find balance.

My new career is where I believe I will find balance in my life. By its very nature of working with dogs and having my own super-energetic dog, I'm much less sedentary. Three years ago, I could be sat on my backside in my car or on a train, at my desk or in a meeting for up to 14 hours a day. 14 hours! Not an occasional thing. I mean most days Monday to Friday. Or working 14 days straight, with long-haul flights, going from Hong Kong to Singapore to Dubai to for property exhibitions. All business class flights and lovely hotels; it sounds so glamorous when you're not doing it. All you want a piece of toast and a good cup of tea on your own sofa.

I still know far too many of my ex-colleagues that are still doing this. This isn't life. Yes, the financial security that I've always coveted like Gollum and the ring, is there. But at too high a price for me.

Taking such a step back financially has been really liberating for me. I had to get used to seeing my savings go down (quite quickly!) rather than my potential retirement pot growing nicely. I've had to get used to that feeling and it is really uncomfortable. But I've been allowing those feelings, accepting them, and realising that nothing amazing happens when you're feeling comfortable.

It's helped me realise that money is far less important to me than I always thought. I know I'm incredibly fortunate to have savings to be able to do this. I've never been much of a spender; I really don't like shopping. But I do crave the feeling of financial peace of mind, the warm blanket of security that it gives me.

Almost exactly 12 months after leaving my well-paid job, and not having paid myself as I invested in my training and my new business, a certain pandemic struck. Ah, the new C-word. The week before, by ridiculous coincidence, I was diagnosed with a bad stress fracture just as all my face-to-face clients were about to disappear. My boyfriend, Ash, always calls me a 'stuffy bitch' – an affectionate Mancunian term for lucky. But I believe to my core I have made my own 'luck' happen.

I'd started walking dogs full time while I was qualifying as a dog trainer. I specifically took on clients' dogs that struggled to find day care or 'normal' dog walkers because their dogs were nervous or reactive to other dogs. A big proportion of these were rescues, which have always been a passion for me.

I'd always planned to have part of my dog training business on-line. Training people in their own homes is the best place to start for the majority of dogs. There are minimal distractions for the dog or puppy and, once the new games are learned at home, they're much more likely to progress quickly when they take these skills outside.

But the combination of studying and dog-walking meant the on-line business development hadn't been moving along quickly enough. You don't earn much money walking dogs one by one, but my inner Gollum was still wanting to pay the bills without eating into my savings too much. I found it far too difficult to turn down paid work, no matter how much I knew it wasn't sustainable (physically and financially).

But, with the pandemic changing the entire landscape, my fledgling business income stopped abruptly.

So with my foot in plaster, and no clients for the time being, it gave me the enforced gift of the time I needed to really start motoring on building up my on-line business.

SOMETIMES A CHANCE HAPPENING CAN SHOW YOU WHAT YOU NEED TO LEARN

6.20am on Friday 28th August 2014 is not a time and date I needed to look up to write this. It was the details on the accident report and moment my life path changed. I was training for a 500 km charity bike ride through Central America, so I used to cycle the 13 miles into central London some days as part of my training.

I got taken out from behind on a roundabout. My bicycle was totalled, and I was bruised and bloody lying in a foetal position on my right side. My helmet was dented, but nothing on me was broken. I was very 'lucky'.

Getting knocked off my bicycle was the catalyst for the biggest change in my life. The physical and emotional effects took over 18 months to fully come to light. But it meant I had to take a hard look at myself. What I valued in life. What I loved in life. What I wasn't capable of anymore. What I <u>was</u> capable of. What I really wanted from my life. It made me realise that I had to make a change with my marriage that was limping along, not giving me anything. That I needed to make a change with my job, and not just because of the crippling anxiety that would flood over me as soon as any kind of stress built up.

My brain wasn't functioning fully. I had a mild brain injury, but at the same time it resulted in the most clarity

I'd ever had. I couldn't carry on as I was. Self-doubt in my mental and physical abilities meant I crumbled; I was at my weakest point. But it meant, stripped back, I was able to see what I wanted to do. And it gave me the absolute confidence to go and grab it, the instant I saw it. No doubts. No thoughts on how I was going to pay the mortgage if it didn't work out. I just knew things had to change and this was what I needed, wanted and could do.

I'm convinced I wouldn't be doing what I'm doing now if I hadn't finally stopped and listened to my heart, and given myself time. I felt horrible panic building in me over several years after the accident. I was faced with the ever-present realisation that I couldn't keep doing what I was doing. I kept trying to keep my head down and just keep going but it was getting harder and harder. I would be in tears all too often in the work loos in the afternoons, or sobbing in the car on the way home. The price I was paying after a day of trying to 'keep everything together'.

For all the fundamental decisions in my life, I have taken several years to reach the right decision. It's like I have to live with potential choices for quite a long time to try them on. Even if it means putting up with the discomfort of living with something that made me really miserable. I was so very scared of making the wrong choice, so my way of dealing with this is to take a really long time to make a decision. I am not saying this is a particularly good decision-making strategy! It's just how things worked out for me. And things really did work out well in the end.

I'm now building my own business, doing something I adore with passion. I've created the business in exactly the shape that I want. I have never been happier, calmer and more fulfilled than I am at the age of 51 at the time of writing this.

I AM INEVITABLE

To my core I'm a very logical person. I like order, I like to know what's going to happen and when. Any major uncertainty leaves me feeling vulnerable. Now this has stood me in good stead my whole career. But it does mean I'm a bit rubbish when it comes to self-reflection and listening to my heart!

I make nearly every decision with sound logical thinking – i.e. my head and not my heart. For career changes I would write detailed lists of pros and cons and carefully weigh everything up before reaching my well-considered opinion. In the end, the most fundamental changes have come when I followed my heart. Deciding to get divorced. Deciding to leave my old career behind and start completely from scratch.

These were the two most pivotal moments in my life that both led to the happiest five years of my life (so far).

To the people that I worked with over the last thirty years, my career change was a massive surprise. They didn't know I was animal-mad. You couldn't keep me away from any friends' dogs. They didn't know that as a kid I thought I was a mini Doctor Doolittle. I would spend hours sitting still waiting for wild squirrels and New Forest ponies to get used to me so that I could hand feed them. The first job I applied for was at the Gweek Seal Sanctuary, after a holiday trip there. As I was only ten I got a lovely letter back saying, 'We'd love to hear from you when you're a bit older.'

I have now built up my dream business of helping dog-lovers believe they can be their dog's best trainer. I fill my days giving people confidence and knowledge to change their dogs' lives for the better. Wherever they are, Pup Talk is there to hold their hand when they are wobbling, listen when they think they're doing a bad job, and give them what they need to have a calm and happy dog.

After a brief spell post-divorce on Tinder (those are stories for a glass of wine and another book), I met the most incredible partner in Ash, five years ago. We couldn't be more different or more complementary. He's been a complete fun-filled Mancunian rock as I wobbled all over the place, struggling to recover from the accident. His belief in me and my abilities is so unwavering, he finally has me believing it myself and everything I am capable of doing.

So, if I could give you one gift, as a thank you for reading this part of my story, I would say listen to your heart: what is it saying? Don't put up with a comfortable 'it's not too bad' life. Embrace what you love and DO something you love. Suddenly, anything feels possible.

In the words of Thanos (Ash is a big Marvel/Avengers fan): 'I am inevitable'.

ABOUT THE AUTHOR

Niki French

Niki French is an animal-mad, people-loving dog trainer. After a thirty-year corporate career, she was in a bicycle accident in 2014 that led her to making a complete life change. It led her back to her childhood dream of working with animals and in 2019 she set up Pup Talk and Twickenham Dog Services. Her 'CEO' is Bodie, a lively young Collie Lurcher Cross from Battersea Cats' and Dogs' Home.

As an internationally successful Sales and Marketing Director, Niki developed and managed teams working on large-scale, UK city centre residential developments, including the Athletes' Village for the London 2012 Olympics.

Niki is now a full-time Pro Dog Trainer, showing dog-owners how to leave stress and frustration behind with simple, fun, and transformational training to help build a stronger bond. Working with owners of many breeds of puppies, nervous rescues and adult dogs with ingrained behaviour problems, Niki gets real life results with easy training games the whole family can play.

Niki is on a mission to give people belief, knowledge, support, and tools to be their dog's best trainer. She believes no dog is beyond help and inspires people to make training an enjoyable part of daily life. Because having a dog shouldn't be hard work.

CONTACT:

Email:
info@puptalk.co.uk
Website:
www.puptalk.co.uk
Facebook free group:
www.facebook.com/groups/puptalk/

facebook.com/puptalk

instagram.com/puptalk101

linkedin.com/in/niki-french-6b6b3a10

twitter.com/puptalk101

16

SARAH GILES

Stepping out of the shadows

Rollback six months to when I was dealing with yet another HR drama, who would have thought I would be now sat in my kitchen contemplating my first ever chapter for a book. The only similarity I can draw on from then is the steaming flat white positioned in front of me.

After a sixteen plus year career in HR, I quit in lockdown. Yes, I resigned from my Head of HR position back in April and left in June. Some might say that was mad during a pandemic. Quite often we get so caught up in our busy lives that we play it safe and stick with what we know. It was finally time for me to step out of my comfort zone.

It has been one heck of a personal development journey getting to this point. For once, I have had time for reflection and to really work out what I want for the future and who I am. I always wanted an HR career and for some reason thought it would mean I had achieved something if I made it. Then I finally got into those leadership roles and realised it was not really for me. It's funny how things turn out, isn't it?

Somewhere I had lost myself through the constant juggle of motherhood and a career. I had been hiding behind my job title and role of mum. I had to start getting to know myself again. It hasn't always been plain sailing, but I've always been quietly determined.

I rediscovered myself, explored what my passions were, invested in myself, and started a whole new adventure. My own coaching journey is partly the reason why I made this change of direction in life.

I hope by sharing my story, I can help you to realise that you already have the strengths within you. It's time to stop standing on the side-lines and step out of the shadows, feel confident owning who you truly are, and take your place in this world as you deserve it too.

"Genius is there in all of us, just waiting for us to tap into it."

— (ROBERT TOTH)

WHERE DID IT ALL START?

Now I'm not going to go back all through my childhood, but I suppose the thing that sticks with me when reflecting is how I started out as that quiet shy girl at school. You know, the one who never wants to put their hand up for fear of getting it wrong. I always had to work hard to get where I wanted to be. I didn't naturally excel at school; I got average grades, but I had to work hard to get them. I was a trier and kept going.

I decided I didn't want to go to university, mostly for fear of taking exams and the worry that I would struggle with it all. It was always my lack of confidence that held me back in the early days. So, I started out in the big wide world of work straight after college and got myself a role at the local council in planning. I really enjoyed it, but after a period of time, I started to feel envious of some of my friends going off to uni. Was I missing out? Was this now my life? Suddenly I wondered if I had made a huge mistake not going to uni. I decided to go back to college part-time and did an HND whilst still working. Then I got promoted and found myself supervising a small team. It was at this point that I found my love of people. Fast forward a couple of years, which is where my HR journey started.

When I started my HR career, I still had the battle of confidence issues and almost dreaded sitting in team meetings. Sometimes I would sit there dying to say something but too afraid to speak up for fear of being judged. I would sit there and just listen to the voices; often people were fighting to be heard. You see, I was a reflector and sat on the side-lines. There were many occasions when I felt like I was never going to get anywhere, being the quiet one. I wasn't quiet when you got to know me, I was just more reserved and wouldn't speak for the sake of it. I didn't feel confident enough to speak up in large groups.

I wouldn't describe myself as introverted, but I have some of the traits; I think I probably sit in the middle. When you don't know me, I can come across more reserved and I don't necessarily seek out social engagements. I mean don't get me wrong, I love a good party when I'm there and having fun, but I'm quite happy in my own company.

I got told so many times by different people I needed to have confidence in my own abilities. I always worked hard and put everything into it. Even when I got fantastic feedback I wouldn't ever stop and recognise it. I didn't like getting compliments; quite frankly I found it embarrassing. But now I'm learning to accept compliments and acknowledge them with a thank you. Why don't you jot that tip down and give it a try?

I was always quietly focused on the next thing I wanted to achieve, but people wouldn't have known I was necessarily ambitious. I found sometimes that when you are quiet you can quite often get overlooked because you don't shout about what you do. Extroverts are often rewarded with promotions into leadership roles, but this doesn't mean they are always going to be the best leaders.

Businesses are really missing something here. I'm not talking specifically about me, but it shouldn't always be about the big personalities and those who stand out from the crowd. Introverts have extremely valuable assets which may help them become exceptional leaders. I don't like putting a label on people, but we should look at the whole person and what they bring to the table. It's not about who shouts the loudest. So, for all you introverts out there, don't worry. You don't have to change your personality to build that self-confidence. I love this quote:

"In a gentle way, you can shake the world."

— (MAHATMA GANDHI)

The next step for me was to start studying for my CIPD (HR qualification) part-time whilst working for a financial services organisation. I met my soul mate, my now-husband Steve. I worked in Southampton during the week and would travel up to London on a Friday and stay most weekends. I got a little taste of city life. Fast forward another year and I had moved in and was working for a top accountancy firm in the city. Oh, those were the days… we certainly had a good social life, lots of dining out, and just making the most of it. However, I'm not sure

I was ever really destined to be the city career woman. It just didn't feel like where I wanted to settle down.

We got engaged in 2008, started our next journey together and bought a house, and got married in 2009. Just over a year later we had our first daughter. Yep, she wasn't far off a honeymoon baby. This is when things started to really change…

THE BALANCING ACT OF WORKING LIFE

Whilst pregnant I was always determined to go back to work. I hadn't quite got to where I wanted to be in my career, and I wasn't going to give up now. Some might say this was selfish. But I knew I would be a better person by trying to get the balance between my career and motherhood. Oh, boy was I in for a shock. Now just to clarify, both Steve and I had never really been around babies nor had any in our family. So, my idea of just breezing through it… well, you can guess where this is going!

I remember us walking through the front door with Millie and just looking at each other. It's scary really when you're suddenly left responsible for this small person. Where was the handbook? There were many ups and downs, but like most parents, we learnt as we went along. We must have done ok as we then had our second daughter, Evie in May 2013. Our family was finally complete!

Juggling an often-frantic HR career whilst caring for a family was certainly a challenge, if not chaotic. Let's face it, being a parent is never easy, whatever your role, but somehow, we get through it. I had to travel quite a bit in one of my roles. I remember commuting to London one day, running the daily gauntlet between nursery drop off and catching the train, with just seconds to spare, and I was looking like a sweaty mess by this point. On this particular day, I managed to lose a shoe between the platform and train, watching in utter horror as the doors closed behind me with only one shoe on board. Honestly, I just wanted to cry but somehow managed to keep it together and it's quite amusing now I look back. I learnt a valuable lesson that day. Always wear flats when travelling. I've had many adventures juggling motherhood and a career. If only we had more time!

For a few years, I just felt like I was on that daily hamster wheel, but I didn't know any different to be honest. As I got higher up in my career there was no time for further development or so I told myself. It's not because I felt I knew everything, more just the lack of time. When I had tried to book a seminar or course, I ended up having to cancel because yet another meeting had been put in my diary.

Steve always worked in London, so it was mostly me juggling the drop-offs and picks up each day. I would often be clock-watching in a meeting at the end of the day and then end up running out the office door so I could beat the traffic. People often use to ask me how I managed as I was always running between meetings, dashing for the kids, working in the evenings, etc, but the reality is lots of women do this. From the outside, I suppose I looked like I had it all together, but the truth is no one has all their shit together! My resilience was certainly tested at times, but the coaching I received as part of my studies really helped me. I just somehow got on with it.

I had quite a regimented routine as there was no time for messing around, especially in the mornings. The evenings would come, and it felt relentless at times with the bedtime routine. Steve and I would eventually sit down for dinner at about eight, and then I'd be on the laptop again working. There was just no let-up some days, so I knew I needed to find some 'me time'.

MY ESCAPE

Whilst trying to get through the juggles of modern life, I knew I needed something to keep me sane. I had always enjoyed running and had trained for some events over the years and always said one day I wanted to do the London Marathon. So, guess what? I entered. I didn't get a ballot place but managed to secure a charity place for Children with Cancer in 2017. So just to be clear, by this point I was in a very busy role, working all hours and juggling children and a home. Why on earth did I then think it would be a good idea to train for a marathon. I don't do things by half!

Off my training started through the winter months in the cold and dark. I only had limited time to go out and train and would often get up on a Saturday at 6am and start my long runs so it didn't eat too much into family time. Anyway, the point of me telling you this is that if you put your mind to something and set goals then you are more likely to achieve them. If I'm completely honest the thought of running some evenings after another crazy day at the office was the last thing I wanted to do, but I did it because I wanted to achieve my goal of completing a marathon.

Although this was a big commitment, it was great for my own mental health. It was my escape even though it was tough at times, but I would always come back feeling good and with a sense of achievement. I suddenly felt physically fitter and better for focusing on my own self-care. When we look after ourselves, we feel good about ourselves and more confident in who we are.

WAS THIS IT?

As I worked my way up into more senior roles, my confidence grew and I finally came out of my shell, feeling comfortable when speaking up. The irony of all of this is having worked so hard to elevate my career to leadership positions, the work I loved was missing. It was never really about the status for me, I was always passionate about supporting the businesses I have worked in and the people in them. The downside to this was that often I wanted to do as much as I could to help others, but it left me over-worked and frazzled at times. Sometimes I wished I could have been one of those leaders who completely switched off and if it didn't get done, they wouldn't lose any sleep over it.

The trouble with working in HR is that you aren't always liked. In fact, you can never do anything right: HR gets blamed for a lot of things. Throughout my career, I've had to do some things I'm not proud of. There were occasions where I've received backlash from angry employees due to the decisions the business had made. They weren't necessarily my decisions, but it was my job to apply them. HR is an emotional rollercoaster! What people don't realise is the emotional strain put on HR professionals today. In all jobs, we get to do the things we enjoy and things we don't like so much. HR is no different. It can be a very lonely place particularly when you move into leadership roles.

This is why resilience is so key for HR professionals. You don't get taught these skills as part of the HR qualifications when you first start in in the profession. This was another reason for me starting to train in wellbeing and resilience. We all know it should be a priority in businesses, but quite often it gets put to the bottom of the pile either because of budgets or the resources to drive it. I wanted to be able to support businesses and HR professionals with this.

When I moved into the leadership roles, I got fed up navigating the politics at the top, even game playing in some businesses. The one thing I just could not stand is when businesses say they act with integrity, but then let their own leaders behave in a way that completely contradicts that. I'm not saying it's always like that, but I have experienced this, and it can be challenging when you're in an HR position.

I have been lucky enough to work with a whole range of leaders throughout my career, some brilliant, and some not so good. Either way, they have all helped shape me into the leader I wanted to be so I'm grateful to have worked with them all.

I QUIT!

In the autumn of 2018, I made the big decision to take the plunge and resigned from my job to set up my own HR consultancy. I wanted to support local businesses whilst giving myself more family time. I was very fortunate that I got some client work through my network, so I hadn't really got to the stage of even setting up a website or going to networking, etc. It all worked perfectly for a time, but if I'm completely honest I was a bit bored. I got approached about an interim contract and got lured back into the professional services world, but I kept telling myself it was temporary, so it was ok.

During this period, I had already started studying a wellness and resilience coaching diploma and started a six-month branding course with Nicki because I always knew deep down, I would go back to doing my own thing. I said earlier I love a challenge, and this certainly provided me with one when hit with a global pandemic alongside a merger, my studies and suddenly home schooling too! Almost immediately the lines between work, home, study, and school were erased and a new era of open chaos descended.

With us both juggling zoom calls/meetings all day it was proving impossible to home-school and work. We did our best but if I'm honest it was total chaos like I'm sure it was in most households. This was really the turning point for me: enough was enough. I had been fortunate to work with some truly great leaders in this business, but I had to put my own needs first.

Was resigning the best option? It was something I had been thinking about for months, and so many scenarios had been playing around in my head. Was now really the best time to lose a good salary? Was it easier to stay where I was comfortable? I really enjoyed the people I worked with and I had built a fabulous team. But there was something inside telling me I needed to do this and now was my opportunity to follow my passion. So, I took the plunge and resigned.

Suddenly it was just me. It's been a bit of a whirlwind journey into entrepreneurship. You see, I didn't want to make the mistakes I did last time. I wanted to truly do something I was passionate about. It's interesting how things change in only a short space of time. It was time to finally do something that set my soul on fire.

I have been through such a journey myself over the last 12 months. I didn't realise at the time how much I had lost myself during my career and being mum. We're always too busy juggling everything that sometimes we don't ever stop. It's sometimes easier to keep doing what we have always done. It took a global pandemic to make me realise that life really is too short. If you know you have more to give and keep putting it off, don't. Why would you want to stop yourself from achieving your goals and dreams? Just something for you to think about.

MY JOURNEY OF SELF-DISCOVERY

How bizarre that I didn't even realise this whole online world of entrepreneurs existed until this point. I did get a bit of a shock when I saw the coaching industry online. I looked up at some big names in the industry and immediately thought maybe I didn't have what it took. I saw these powerful women out there being bold and visible. I knew I wasn't going to make it if I didn't start getting visible myself. I realised I had some limiting beliefs and did a mindset course to help me with this. During this course, I realised this was something that my clients would really benefit from and so my NLP journey began.

For those of you that don't know, NLP stands for Neuro-Linguistic Programming. It provides practical ways in which you can change the way you think, view past events, and how you approach life. In my resilience studies, I had already done some work around mindset, but I wanted to learn some techniques which I could use with my clients. I then got certified as an NLP practitioner and Break-through Coach.

By this point, I had a lot of time for self-reflection and I reminded myself about the progress I made in my career. It is easy when you start out in business doing something different to forget about all your past skills and experiences you bring to the table. When I started out in my HR career, I was always looking up at the HR Directors and thinking, *"one day I want to be in that role"*, but I wanted to do it my way. And to some degree that's what I did. I have always stayed true to who I am as a person. If it meant I wasn't going to reach those leadership roles, then I was ok with that. But deep down I was always quietly ambitious, just never one to shout about it. I no longer needed a title to hide behind!

At this point, I got a little bit addicted to personal development and have really invested not only in myself but also
to support my clients the best I can. I've gone on to train
in Timeline Therapy, Energy work, Positive Psychology,
and there's more on the list. When I first started training
in wellbeing and resilience, I didn't even think about
having to be coached myself. Sometimes we are often
scared of doing that inner work, but it's been a fantastic
journey. It's helped me to find my purpose and what I'm
truly passionate about. When you start believing in yourself you take action.

This journey certainly hasn't been an easy one though.
When I first came into the online space (and let's face it
this year we had no choice), I found it exhausting seeing
all the social interaction and live videos etc. I could quite
happily have gone and hidden away. But then I reminded
myself that I got on in my career by staying true to who I
was, so why couldn't I now. Yes, we talk lots about being
visible in business, but we can do it in a way that works for
us and in a way we're comfortable with. Sometimes you
must remind yourself to stay on your own path and not
get distracted by others. I truly believe you can do it in
your own way.

And so, my coaching business was born. I had managed to
finally step out of the shadows, and I wanted to help
others do the same.

I'm sat here with another flat white reflecting back over the years. I don't regret not leaving the corporate world sooner. I think everything we do in life teaches us new experiences which lead us on to the next. Starting my own coaching journey really allowed me that time for self-reflection and to finally see it was ok to get off the hamster wheel, strip away the title, and get to know myself again.

MY ADVICE: FROM ME TO YOU.

If you ever feel you still have more to give, but fear or low self-confidence is holding you back then my advice is to go for it. Don't put a limit on your own abilities. Some of the most successful people are the ones who failed many times before they succeeded. If you are feeling stuck and unsure where you're heading, then start by reconnecting with yourself and doing that inner work.

We often try to create that perfect life by changing our outside environment thinking we will finally be the person we want to be. The truth is, you won't change you as a person until you are prepared to start working on yourself and letting go of what's in your way.

"The scariest moment is always just before you start."

— (STEPHEN KING)

We live in busy times and sometimes we think we must do more just to keep up. We then end up putting ourselves at the bottom of our to-do list. You have to learn to slow down and find that time to reconnect with yourself. Things won't seem so scary when you are truly aligned with your passions and values. It's only when you start believing in yourself that the magic really starts to happen. If I can do it then I know you can too. It's not selfish to want to be the best version of you. When you live confidently you open yourself up to opportunities.

Here's another quote I love.

"Look fear straight in its ugly face and barge forward."

— (HELEN MIRREN)

We've all had those moments when we'd rather run from what's happening than face it. We pretend that the problem will just go away and put if off for another day. Sometimes you have to face what lies behind those doors and often it isn't as bad as you first thought. It's totally worth it when you come out the other side. It's a journey but just start taking baby steps and don't quit. You will soon step into your potential and show the world a confident you.

ABOUT THE AUTHOR

Sarah Giles

Sarah Giles is a confidence & mindset coach for quietly ambitious women with purpose. Sarah helps them to step out of the shadows, unlock their natural strengths and make an impact as their true self. She uses a blend of coaching and NLP techniques to support her clients on their transformation journey.

Sarah also works with organisations offering bespoke 1:1 and group coaching to support with employee wellbeing. Providing people with the tools to help make some positive changes to enhance their health and wellbeing.

Sarah is passionate about coaching others to build the confidence and resilience to be their best self and step into their potential.

Sarah has a background in HR spanning over sixteen years and has operated in a variety of roles leading up to Head of HR/HR Director level. She has experienced numerous industries but spent most of her time working in Professional Services.

Sarah is a Chartered Member of the Institute for Personnel & Development, a certified NLP (Neuro-Linguistic Programming) Practitioner, Life Coach and Time Line Therapy Practitioner. She is also qualified in Psychometric testing and uses a variety of Resilience and Strengths profiling tools in her work.

CONTACT:

Website: www.sarah-giles.com

facebook.com/sarahgilescoaching

linkedin.com/in/s-giles

instagram.com/sarah_giles_coaching

17

SARAH SHEARMAN

Less Dickhead, More Awesome!

I am a high ID. For those of you wondering what the hell I am talking about, it is my DISC profiling. A high ID. Only the second personality profile test I had taken (that I remember).

Description:

*People with the **ID** (Influencer/Direct) personality type tend to be energetic and adventurous, communicating with casual language, bold statements, and a focus on the big picture. They are likely to have an easy, relaxed, casual manner when speaking or interacting with others and enjoy the challenge of meeting new people.*

Typically known for their social skills, creativity, and charisma, they can clearly and vividly appeal to others using an emotionally expressive and demonstrative style, often able to convince them to take action.

Strengths

- *Trusting intuition and ability to improvise.*
- *Using positive, enthusiastic verbalisation when motivating others.*
- *Quickly spotting new opportunities for advancement.*
- *Solving problems by involving others in brainstorming and open discussion.*
- *Delegating responsibility for detailed tasks.*
- *Bringing energy and a sense of adventure to a team.*
- *Placing a high priority on personal interactions and relationships.*
- *Creating novel solutions to challenging problems.*

Weaknesses

- *Struggling to follow predictable routines.*
- *Failing to evaluate problems realistically due to overly optimistic expectations.*
- *Pursuing too many new ideas at once.*
- *Winning people over, even when they have a more logical argument.*
- *Trying to control all of the results.*
- *Stepping too far out of the details of important projects.*
- *Creating an environment that is too flexible for people who need a structured approach to work.*
- *Having the inability to limit time spent interacting with people.*

That was in early 2019. Since then I have completed at least four more personality profile tests.

Personality tests have been a huge part of my personal development journey and they have become significant stepping-stones to creating success within my business because I have learned to manage me effectively. They were the gift of truly understanding who I am and with that knowledge came the confidence that I needed to own my strengths and play them to my advantage. It has stopped me from feeling guilty about delegating, helped to identify where I need to set my set boundaries and why I need to protect them. Now I can recognise who is positive for me and who is toxic. The insight has been invaluable so far on this path of self-discovery and key to me reaching my goals. The tests have been the realisation that I have spent a majority of my forty years not fully knowing or understanding me. It hit home to me even more so in the past 18 months. Acceptance has at last arrived but the search for self-love and fulfilment continues.

When the opportunity to write and be part of a collaborative book landed on my lap as a result of signing up to a business mastermind group, I stumbled on what to write about because in truth I don't see myself as a success (YET!), so the very real imposter syndrome has a hold of me tightly and the mind monkeys are playing fruitful games of deceit.

Who am I? Who am I to think of being 'good' enough to be part of a book? You're not a writer… who wants to listen to you going on? Yep, all that stuff has been playing on repeat the past few weeks.

With the ever-approaching deadline to submit my chapter, I chucked some nuts and bananas their way to quieten them and decided to draw on what others say about me, because being the trusting type, I am starting to believe them and all the super things I keep getting told.

So, let me take you on a journey that starts from a place of lost desperation hugging on to some bold, albeit fake, confidence with one arm, while gripping a bucket of hope, weirdly misplaced energy and optimism in the other. It is a long road full of emotional ditches mostly powered by good tunes, hot men and new shoes as I succumb to my celebrity money mindset personality. A mirrored path with moments of reflections as I step into many different identities. A story of change and choice.

I mention this because, honestly, I used to be a bit of a d!ckhead. I am not proud of that fact but I am grateful for this path of learnings and opportunities, proud of the choices I have made to get me to this place which is filled with a whole lot more awesomeness and much less of the d!ckheadishness (I'd say just 5% now).

It's ok if you are a bit of a d!ck or have been before – there is always time to change, be better, do good and find your happy place. No new year's resolutions needed here. Just an open mind and curious soul.

If you want to stop dimmering and you are ready to start shining yourself about for you and those around you to prosper, then see if you like what I have to say. You might find it inspiring, that's my hope anyhoo.

(I realise that d!ckheadishness, dimmering and anyhoo are not officially real words, but what can I say – I am the Nicole Scherzinger of Essex. Don't be shocked if I make up some more words as we go along).

It makes sense to start at the beginning of young adulthood:

Identity 1

1996 - 2000

16-20 years old

The tearaway teenager turned young Mum to single parent

I was sixteen when I walked into the JD Sports store in Romford that was to change my life. It was here I got my first job and I met my first serious boyfriend, seven years older than me and in my parents' eyes, trouble. They had encouraged me to get a job because I had my first trip booked to go abroad with my friends, a girly trip to Tenerife and they had agreed to pay for the trip if I got a job to cover the spending money. My parents were generous to me, too generous. I was spoilt, learned the way of instant gratification and had an obvious lack of financial management skills.

The holiday came and went and was my first eye opener to drinking games, the strip of bars that boozy destinations like Playa De Las Americas generally have and the all-round chaos that comes with that type of holiday. I loved it. Having partied from a young age, quite often illegally, this side of the party scene came as a surprise. I had never seen people swapping clothes, drinking beer from the bottle with socks over them, passing balloons intimately between each other's bodies or racing to do ten different sex positions in pairs. Games, wild, wild games. Young, drunk and sex mad (mostly teenagers) living what they thought to be their best life. The buzz, the energy, the craziness, the music, the laughs. I revelled in it.

From the title of this chapter maybe you expect the next part of the story to go like this... I cancelled my return flight home, stayed for the whole season as a rep for one of the bars on the strip and came home pregnant by a barman I had a fling with. Well, that wasn't quite the path I was meant to take. Already in love with my boyfriend, I headed home.

After this trip and six months into college, having picked my subjects - politics, psychology and law with the ambition then to become a barrister - I was told by the lecturer that people like us from this social class rarely make it in this profession. I didn't need much more persuasion to quit on my studies. Applying myself academically has always been a struggle. I am smart enough, just too fidgety in my personality, and here was an easy exit. I started working full time in retail, followed by moving out of my parents' and shortly after that was pregnant with my first child. I was seventeen.

July 1998, my son was born.

Now eighteen, we bought our first home and for a while we were working at a financial organisation together. It was the start of his career path to success but for me it had a different lesson. I was temping there in the call centre, when the chance to apply for a permanent role came up. I jumped on it and sat the entry test alongside a friend from college. I failed. The not so resilient, unprepared me received the message loud and clear. I am not clever enough for the corporate world. There were lots of tears and I headed back to the retail world, a place where I felt safe and worthy. It was the beginning of untapped potential being buried.

For the first two years I took well to motherhood. A stable relationship and a nice home helped keep me on an even keel, but true contentment and happiness didn't live here with our family. Riddled with insecurity, overwhelmed by the responsibility of parenthood and adulting, and just generally lost, I fled the relationship and moved back to my parents with my two-year-old boy.

Full of bitterness at the wrongdoings of my partner, I took the stance of blame, blame, blame. It was all my parents' fault. They should have stopped it, they could have guided me better, they should have raised me to be able to cope and manage in life. That was the easiest way to avoid taking no or little responsibility for my own actions. I knew best. It was here I entered the next phase of life.

Identity 2

2000 – 2008

20-28 years old

The serial girlfriender and unwanted friend

Straight into a toxic relationship, I dated a guy for just under a year and had my first experience of the stereotypical awful mother-in-law. My god, she hated me. Her two grown boys were her world and me with child in tow made her feel threatened. I will never forget the conversation I had with her in her very large and posh kitchen. *You and my son will never be together; he deserves better than you. He shouldn't have to raise someone else's kid. I want him to get married and have his own kids and if you think he will be leaving this house to be with you at Christmas, well, that won't be happening.* This episode has stayed with me for a long time. It made me feel like damaged goods. For a while I stayed in the relationship in spite of her.

Luckily for me, I had two more long term positive relationships that followed. Eighteen months in I was engaged to the next guy, followed in quick succession by a four-year relationship with an awesome guy. We lived together and he was just amazing to me and was a brilliant step dad. Our relationship broke down: there were causes on both sides but actually it was more me. I was in self-destruction mode. I was jealous, insecure, lost, depressed, having problems with friends and in a huge amount of debt.

During this time my main group of friends fell apart around me. I was the centre of a big drama. The leader of the pack didn't invite me to the day part of her wedding, I was the only one cast out. Up until this point every birthday, hen party, day at the races, wedding was attended as a consolidated group regardless of the alliances to the host that was inviting for the particular event. There were reasons but all just poor excuses to make her actions acceptable. Despite my true friends being in agreement with me, there was nothing they could do. It was after all her wedding.

I was livid and boy, did they know. I went mad. They should be sticking up for me was the thought at the forefront of my mind. I felt rejected and in complete despair, my actions were irrational and silly. From embarrassment I walked away from the whole group, including my best friends. Thinking of this time brings tears to my eyes. I was heartbroken and rejected. I suffered in silence watching on at the lives of the conjoined friendships via social media. For a long time the subliminal message was *you don't belong*. This event marred my following friendships in the years to come and to this day I still struggle in any group set up. Triggered easily, the sabotaging thoughts lead to destructive behaviours, which quite often means any group environments are temporary for me. It feels heavy to constantly carry the desire to belong.

I was back home at my parents again, single, unstable, and unsure. I left the world of retail work (at this point I was at managerial level) and entered the office world. Still lost, still not taking ownership for my actions, feeling a little more broken, and the underlying hurt was presented in the form of anger, selfishness and narcissism.

Identity 3

2008 – 2011

28 – 31 years old

The City Girl and Serial Dater

My big break came after two years temping to build up my office skills. I got a job on a trading floor at an investment bank. A friend recommended me for the desk assistant role and wow, just wow. The opportunity of a lifetime. It was professional, cool, in the city, with more money than I had ever had. This was the stepping-stone to a successful career and the building blocks of becoming a business owner. It came hand in hand with a great social life and lots of flings of dating. Having partied the past eight years as the designated driver (lack of funds but a desire to go out led to a practically teetotal life on the rave scene) I now had access to socialise, quite often on someone's corporate card and being just a train ride from home meant I didn't need to worry about the expense of a cab or need the convenience of my car. This resulted in me drinking. I remember a few times my dad bailing me out with a 2am pick up from a station far from home because I had once again missed my stop. He would arrive to a rather drunk Sarah in a heap of tears and emotion saying, *no one loves me, I hate myself, why do I have to be this way? I want to be 'normal'.*

Despite these episodes and many soul destroying messers badged up as men, my confidence grew in leaps and bounds as I navigated this educated land of luxury living and middle classism. I was battling with feeling inferior but my charismatic entrepreneurial way saw me through. It was a contract role: after six months I got a permanent role at another bank. It was 2008, just before the recession hit. I was lucky to get one of the last employed jobs available that year.

Three years in and I had formed a group of circumstantial friends. They all had groups of friends outside of work so my neediness for attention from them was apparent.

Then the career leap. I moved to an interdealer brokers into a sales role. With no prior knowledge or experience I launched a volume matching IRS electronic trading screen to nearly 400 traders across 39 banks in 6 countries in just 4 months! Let me just break that shit down so you can truly appreciate how epic it was for me.

I had to learn about the fixed income market, I had to learn about interest rate swaps as a trading product, why they are traded, who trades them and how. Then I had to learn the trading screen, its functionality, the project development plan and a sales pitch. Met all the brokers on the desk, train them how to use the platform. After all of that I then had to manage seeing all of the traders, the travel arrangements and the feedback from them to the business heads, project and development team as well as make sure the traders were all onboarded. Finally launch the thing. It was a success and, in that company, I went from strength to strength. Promoted was a dirty word in the flat structure of the organisation, but for me a move to business manager and later project manager felt like a step up each time. During these years I passed the financial rules and regulations exam and qualified in PRINCE II (a project management methodology). Since starting in the city, on a generous level of earning I went on to more than double my salary over the eight years working there. Go ME!

Identity 4

2012

32 years old

The Bad Mum

There are many quotes around regrets. Mostly they encourage you not to have them and instead take away the experience and lesson. I try my best to live by this kind of motto when reviewing the decisions that I have made. Telling myself I did my best at that time with the knowledge, tools and skills I had in that moment.

But there is one decision that will forever live in my heart with the feeling of regret. There is no avoiding it, no flipping it over to the positive side.

It was In 2011, so desperate to be loved, accepted and part of something, that I fell in love, not just with the guy but with his family and with the feeling of security that he gave me. His intentions were clear early on that I was his 'one', so I guess I also fell in love with the idea of a forever.

The relationship between him and my son was tense and uncomfortable. It was not insightful adult mentality vs child logic facing up against each other; instead, he had a fundamental hatred for blended families and a complete avoidance of embracing the role of step dad, versus a teenager that didn't feel welcome in his own home, that felt vulnerable sensing danger ahead and a lack of support from his mum.

The clash grew bigger along with the wedge between a mother and her child and their already fragile bond. A move to his father's was agreed. There could be no winner. A rejected son, a heartbroken mum and a man that thinks he has won his prize possession, but actually he was gifted an unseen seed of resentment.

I should have been stronger. I should have protected him. I hope to rebuild, but until then I'll live with a very raw emotion that is regret.

Identify 5

2013

33 years old

The Wife

Finally, I belonged. I was part of my very own super team, one half of a duo. was getting married which meant I had a built-in adventure buddy for life. I was in my element with the whole thing, the dress, the event, the planning, and being creative making whatever I can. Smiling like a Cheshire cat springs to mind. Ask any of the attendees from the invites to the after party, it went down as one of the best weddings they had attended. Ibiza as a destination definitely gave me a helping hand but I will take the legend party planner title for this event, because it was fricking awesome. Swept up in the moment is an understatement.

As the age old (yet modern) saying goes, a marriage is more than the wedding day. The last piece of glitter had fallen, return flights boarded, the dress dry cleaned, name changed, new passport arrived and it was off to the honeymoon we went. A road trip around Europe. The not yet obvious cracks that were forming pre-wedding started to show signs; our polar opposite personalities and coping mechanisms for life and approaches to situations caused frictions and conflicts for most of our time away. Head over heels in love, I brushed them off.

It's only now that I can see in my later years that I have a slight attraction to negative, narcissistic men. It is a weird thing and to make sense of it I can only describe it as an urge to spread my happy vibes to them. really feel their struggles and want to dive right in and relieve them of them. It's like my cup is overflowing with love so I want to pour it all over them as if trying to drown their problems.

Eager to take the 'Mrs' title but unaware that this particular identity, despite how contractual and committed in its nature, was only giving me a quick fix of belonging. The security that I yearned for needed to come from within rather than the arms of another and my journey of self-love was not even on the agenda at this time. The gaping hole inside of me was still open. Previous relationships had provided a sheer cover. The marriage was more of a bridge, albeit wobbly, but very much a temporary measure.

Blinded by the current badge of honour, I went steaming full speed ahead, filling the shoes of wifey.

Identity 6

2014 - 2017

34 – 37 years old

The Triplet (plus 1) Mum aka uncertified supermum

Summer 2014 we got the earth-shaking news that there were three gestational sacs, each one with a beating heart clearly displayed on the screen as the result of the ultrasound. Just moments before entering the room I was bawling my eyes out in the waiting area in anticipation of being told I had miscarried. That's why we were there getting an early scan organised by my very caring doctor. The bleeding had started a week after the positive pregnancy test.

The scene went like this

Doctor: Is this an IVF pregnancy?

Me: No

Doctor: Well, there are definitely two sacs that I can see

Me: silent as the doctor turns the screen. I can see a third sac very clearly on the screen.

Doctor: there is a third sac but we will need to do an internal scan to see if there is a heartbeat because I cannot see it here.

Internal scan completed.

IT WAS TRIPLETS!

Well, there were very mixed emotions as we told our family: amazement, disbelief, joy, panic. I could go on. For a while I was a little unsure about this. In all honestly, I was gutted in the first instance. I can see how that comes across as ungrateful, something I have felt guilty for feeling but it turns out it's actually a common thing to think and feel for women expecting multiples.

The pregnancy went extremely well. At the twelve-week scan in the UCL hospital we were given a lot more information about triplet pregnancy, including the risks and the option to reduce to twins or a singleton. We decided it was all or nothing. As you can imagine it was a stressful countdown of weeks to their arrival, knowing the survival rate for each milestone.

Bearing the weight of three babies until 35+4 weeks (I literally couldn't stand for long and was in a wheelchair by the end), the c section was booked and three healthy babies were born.

My friends always talk about the large whiteboard I had to monitor the nappies, sleep, food intake and medicine. We used to get asked so many questions about the babies it was impossible to keep up with who had pooed, had wet nappies and had drunk enough milk. With lots of love and support from family and friends, a great routine from the hospital, we nailed it at the beginning.

I am known as the 'triplet mum'. I have a love-hate relationship with this as an identity for me. Of course I am extremely proud of this title, of course I love my children dearly; we made a decision to go all in on having three and it was without a doubt the right choice; however, here I am the 'super' mum and in all parenting scenarios I become a little alienated, because now I am either misunderstood or my family set up is incomprehensible or my laid back and fairly organised approach makes them feel inadequate. I used to dream about how nice it would be to be part of one of those NCT mummy groups, where our kids all grow up together, we do cool holidays, baby raves, mums nights out, dads nights out, summer BBQs together – that was all squashed at that early scan too!

It's not just that though: once people know something big like this about you, sometimes it's the only thing that they then see, as if it's all that defines me. So yes, I am a loud and proud triplet mumma, in fact it is often the thing I mention first but I will happily take other labels, in particular, business bombshell.

Six months into parenthood, I said, 'Hey, hubby, I've got some news. You remember that one time we had sex this year? Well, turns out you really have super sperm... I'm pregnant!' He definitely wasn't winning any Mr Happy awards on that day.

When she arrived, the triplets were just fifteen months old. We had four babies in nappies, unable to do much for themselves. It was chaos but having her shifted something in me. I felt like I had missed out the first-time round with my eldest being such a young mum and not cherishing our years together. Having the triplets made me feel like that again because we were only just surviving keeping them alive. It was hard to relish in the cute moments because there was always another baby with a need. We were knee deep in bottles, baby linen, car seats, super-sized prams and goo goo gaa gaa. With her, the now baby of the family, not only did the family feel complete (I am a sucker for an even number) but I got some one-to-one time. It made it all feel a bit more normal, just having one baby to care for. I could escape the realities of triplets to go and breastfeed her or when they were at preschool, we could do the just mum and baby thing.

Looking back over these five years and all the memories we have made makes me emotional. It's been tough but we have given them a great life so far and I love that our house is noisy. It's a social hub with friends, family and helpers coming and going all the time.

As you can imagine, kids put pressure on all relationships. The stress of four children in fifteen months would take its toll on any couple. Unfortunately, ours was not to pass the test.

Identity 7

The Divorcee & Single Parent

We called it quits on the marriage Summer 2019. It had been brewing for years though. Already emotionally detached from each other, he moved out. Completely unprepared for the grief that followed his departure and baffled by longing for something I no longer wanted, it knocked me off balance and for a long time I was unable to get back up. He was my security blanket, his family were my comforter and our little family unit was my dream. It was the right choice but the adjustment took its toll on my mental health. Missing what we had and what we were due to build sent me into deep depression. Through the years I had denied that I suffered with bouts of feeling low but this time it took a firm grip. For months I was unmotivated, unproductive, spent my days without the kids in bed and just couldn't focus. The support of medication and weekly counselling helped me navigate back to some kind of normality, but time really is a good healer. For someone impatient like me this road of recovery felt long.

Being a single mum is a badge I have worn before. Twenty years older and after many more children, this time round it is more taxing as you would expect, wearing on my energy. This new path still needs some work but determination and resilience keep us on track as we navigate our new family dynamic.

Identity 8

Sarah The Business Owner, Positive Disruptor

It's been a crazy decade....

After the kids, I tried to go back to my city working life but it was the catalyst of months of panic attacks. A high-pressured job that was long hours didn't fit with a young family. Despite suffering from the anxiety, I am extremely grateful for it because even though the small flickering desire I had to make my own waves in this world, I had never braved a path of business. Lack of courage and self-belief had held me back. The kids and an inflexible city work life balance ignited my dreams to create an organisation that can do good for this world and help me make money while doing it. Proudly, I can say I am a business owner and it was within me all along. It was meant to be. What was that advert that used the line *the future looks bright?* This perfectly describes how I feel in this moment. It has made me resiliently happy, helped me learn about me, my why, my purpose and good habits that have given me many coping mechanisms to manage the trials and tribulations of life (well most of the time!).

So here we are in 2020. The past decade has been crazy for me, with so many learnings.

Being vulnerable and open about my story has brought me more understanding of myself, closer to belonging than I could ever have imagined. My business network and the circle of friends is a credit to me and shows the huge journey I have taken. There are no more toxic relationships, just supportive amazing friendships, wholesome and genuine filled with love. I am extremely lucky.

Personality profiling has brought me to a place of acceptance. Allowing me to recognise my awesomeness and truly embrace who I am, boldly and proudly. Emancipating me from callousness to a point of realisation that grey exists; compassion, understanding and empathy are required. You can always be kinder, less selfish and way less dickhead.

Bring on the next decade

Personally, there is still room for growth, as I continue on the last few pieces of my puzzle; making *me* my secure base, with rock solid self-love, instilling discipline for good habits, creating my own financial independence and freedom from the self-sabotaging thoughts that I have been so used to.

Love and connection are a key driver for me. I am desperate to be loved. Just letting the universe know here that I will be ready for wholesome and genuine love, keep an eye out for all the steps I am taking to get me there. I don't need another lesson relationship; I am ready for the real thing.

As I learn to move from co-dependent to independent, as I develop a true and deep self-love of Sarah and as I master the destined role of a maverick that is ready for me, I expect breathtakingly good things to happen. There are very big plans in the making, to bring integrity to the front of the queue and make business a kinder place where giving back is second nature because doing good is good for business.

Sarah Shearman, Growth Specialist

Sarah Shearman is the business bombshell shaking up the trades world with her hands on, pragmatic approach to business.

After a successful career in the city, Sarah knows all too well the struggles of producing under pressure, and when she was dealt the life card of triplets unexpectedly in 2015, the juggle of a young family and the corporate job took its toll on her personal wellbeing, and led her to a place of self-discovery.

Having always been passionate about helping people, it wasn't until she escaped the hustle and bustle of inner-city life that Sarah realised how she could hone her why and purpose, and use them to help others.

Combining the love for all things business, her innovative nature, project management and leadership skills, Sarah launched Sway Evolve, a one stop shop business management consultancy that focuses on getting her business owners off the tools and working with the clients they love.

Sarah's modern approach to business growth bridges the gap between consulting and coaching, creating the perfect catalyst for lasting change. Calling on an army of top specialists in various niches and specialisms, Sway Evolve is helping business owners not only realise their full potential, but fulfil it with the full support of a team of industry specialists at their side.

Having overcome her own personal battles, Sarah openly shares her story of loneliness, grief, depression and anxiety with the aim to inspire others to be brave and bold and step into their own shoes of business leader that they want to be.

CONTACT:

Sarah@swayevolve.com
https://www.instagram.com/swayevolve/
https://www.instagram.com/myarmyoflittlepeople/

facebook.com/swayevolve

instagram.com/_sarahshearman

linkedin.com/in/saraheshearman

18

SONAL DAVE

People Like YOU Don't Go Very Far..........

What do they mean by "YOU", and who are these people that don't go very far? Who actually has the right to say that!

The truth from my perspective, is that it doesn't matter what you are like, where you come from and how far you go. It's your life, your ambitions and importantly your choice. No one should decide that for you.

I would like to think that an individual would take the time to get to know someone before making such comments but unfortunately this was not the way it was. It was all about what they saw, the colour of my skin and that I was different. I think they may have been scared as I was different from what they knew and understood. Their own prejudices or ones that were forced on them. They did not want to listen to me or hear me and at times it felt like they did not even see me. I know I am petite and 4ft 9 but I should be heard, seen and listened to. I knew this was wrong on so many levels but at this stage, I just did not know what to do. The hard part was that I realised I was the "YOU".

To be honest, this was such a shame, and actually a loss to them, as I knew I had so much to offer. I was prepared to put in the hard work because that's what I do. I didn't smoke or drink coffee so I was at a desk most of the day ready to work hard and do the jobs others did not want to do.

You often hear stories of discrimination and being treated differently but I never thought it could happen to me. How wrong I was. People just do not get it and very often will not even know that they are discriminating. In fact, if you told them they were they would get defensive and irate. There is so much education that is still needed and we all need to play a part in this to tell our stories and educate others. Especially those who just do not get it.

I'm going to take you on a little journey of what life was really like in my career. This includes both the highs and the lows with the various challenges I faced. It was definitely a scary roller coaster at times and one I would not want to go through ever again, although if I did I think I might react differently now.

Some of you might resonate with my story and some of you might be triggered. Some of you might be thinking, "No way, that can't have happened again, again and again." Unfortunately, it did happen many times, but also bear in mind this all started back in 1992, a number of years ago. However, those years have not been forgotten and never will. I'm not sure Optimum Bias was even heard of then but it was definitely there and felt on a regular basis.

I want you to step back and put yourself in the position of the manager and then you, as a member of staff at the time. It would be great to know what you think and feel?

I'm not going to lie to you. It was tough back in those days. As an Indian woman you were supposed to keep your head down and do what you were told. You were not supposed to have a voice or an idea. The thought of wanting a career and climbing the management ladder was laughed at. I suppose what made it harder back then was this thought of keeping your head down and getting on with your work was expected both in the workplace and also at home. I am an Indian woman, I am the middle sibling and I am from the BAME community. This should not get in the way or make it harder for me to follow my career, my dreams and my passions.

Through my chapter, I'm going to show you that even when the toughest try to bring you down you can still rise above and shine bright. These barriers that humans put in place were made to be broken down, or you could just crash through as that might be fun as well. Remember, it's human's who put up these barriers and you are one as well, so you have the right to remove them.

My story starts in Uganda, Jinja in 1968. I was born to my loving parents who found out very quickly through diagnosis, that I had congenital hip dysplasia. This is where the twists and turns that we call challenges made their way into my world for the first time. Yes, as a baby.

Now my special unique version of events for Uganda is that Idi Amin was feeling a little bit nervous and threatened by us Indians, thinking we were going to take over what he called "his country". He asked, well actually, he told all Indians that they had to leave the country by a certain date. I luckily had already come to the UK as a baby in my mum's arms so I did not get to feel or hear the fear, but the stories I have heard make me realise that it was a very unpleasant time trying to get out of the country with what you could and anything you left behind you chose to forget about. Not sure what happened to those Indians that did not manage to get out but I hope they managed to get into hiding and were safe.

I can't remember the exact date but I know it was in 1992. I had come back from travelling and needed a job. I think I'd had a one or two months short term contract that had finished and I was back at the Job Centre looking for work. I remember this tall Asian guy, for the purpose of this part of the story we shall call him Bob, walk towards me and ask me to join him at his desk.

I was just talking about potential next jobs and how tough it was when he asked me if I would like to work at the Job Centre? Looking back I wonder if he was asking me because he genuinely wanted to offer me a job at the Job Centre or maybe he liked me as he was smiling a lot and leaning in, who knows? But anyway, I said yes, and to be quite honest I said yes because if I'd said no it would've looked bad, right? So I said yes. That was the three-month casual job which turned into twenty-plus very long years.

The job was good and Bob and I did get on well and when a full-time post was coming up he told me to apply. If I am honest with myself, it was not the job I wanted. I wanted to be an actress, a performer and singer plus travel around the world but I needed a job. It was that or the potential of the marriage and settling down conversation-starting and I did not want that. I knew that if I wanted to live life my way then I would need to work.

We are now a year on from the casual job and I am in my full-time role. Yes, you read that right. I got the job. I was working in a Job Centre doing basic admin duties and reception work. I was kept away from what was called the "real work" as I was told, **"you had to be in a post for**

a long time before you would have the skills to do the more difficult work". This work was taking claims for people, so gathering information and filling in forms to help them or reviewing forms they had already completed. So that's talking, listening, writing and reviewing. Do you know what, I can hear you already saying "really, that can't be right, that's not too difficult." Well that was exactly what I was told!

A colleague in the office, we will call her Janice, decided that I was well and truly capable and she started to show me the ropes and what would happen during the taking of a new claim, not just booking in people for appointments so a bit more autonomy. On one particular day, Janice was going to let me sit in on one of the claims that she was taking.

I was really excited and I remember sitting next to her when she said: "I just need to get something from the printer". Anyway, the printer was upstairs so she left and then she didn't come back. So it was like five minutes, ten minutes and I had a client sitting in front of me and I just did not really understand what was going on. I thought to myself, oh well, I know what to do. How hard can it be? I will just start taking the new claim and that's exactly what I did. I went through the whole form, got their signature and as they were leaving, Janice popped her head around the corner from coming down the stairs and said: "I knew you could do it". Now that made me smile for days after but it did make me wonder why Janice could see the potential in me and not others. Was it because she herself had been through what I was now going through? I would love for you all to be like Janice and look for the possibilities and opportunities in each other and not let fear or competition be your driver.

Of course, now having these new skills, I was ready to go. I had a flame inside me that wanted to glow bright and be given lots of new energy. My time had started. I requested that I get involved with a bit more high-level work because I was finding I was finishing my work quickly and I was starting to get a little bored. This was when I got the response that will stay with me for always. I am sure at the time I was hurt by what they said but probably did not fully understand the meaning. You know the response already but I am going to remind you what was said to me, **"people like you don't go very far."** I bet people would think twice before saying that today.

Many years went by and with every little chip away at me to make me fall and break, I grew stronger. I had applied for jobs taking me up the career ladder and got the jobs. I was becoming a force to be reckoned with but the challenges and being treated differently never quite went away. Internally, I was feeling angry, frustrated and just wanted to scream out loud but externally my ambition and drive to break down barriers and try new things was my driving force to get to where I wanted to get to regardless of other outdated thoughts and opinions. I had learnt the art to always smile as if everything was ok and this scared people.

There was this one occasion when Sally (not her real name of course), had recently become my manager and she'd asked me to review a document for her. I did the review and collated my feedback and sent back my thoughts. It was nothing too horrific or too disastrous but it was my thoughts on potential changes or minor errors I had spotted. This is what she had asked me to do. I gave her the feedback on her document and left the office for the day. Two days later I was summoned to her office for a meeting. The response I got from Sally was **"if you don't like what I've written, don't agree with what I've written. If you can find fault with what I've written then maybe this job isn't for you."** You can imagine how shocked I was. As I left her office I was gobsmacked. Did she just say that? What did I do wrong? A host of questions that I just did not have answers to and I was not going to get any answers from Sally. This was not supposed to be so hard. I knew I was not stupid so why was this happening to me?

This nicely takes me to a quote that I am sure you will all understand:

"The single biggest problem in communication is the illusion that it has taken place."

— *GEORGE BERNARD SHAW*

So what does this actually mean? Misunderstanding and confusion will often happen because you have thought you have said something when actually what you have only done is thought about them. Often, the reader or listener is having to read between the lines and understand what you are thinking or wanting to say but if you do not clearly say or state what you want people to hear, how can you expect them to understand. It's the illusion, the grey area that will cause the problems.

You might now be thinking that there can't be any more, Sonal. I wish I could tell you that there wasn't. It just did not seem to stop. It was like I had a target on my head. It was awful and at times I wanted to give up and resign but then I would sleep on it and wake up remembering that I was a survivor.

I had decided that I was going to try and go to the big league as I had seen a vacancy for the role of an Assistant Director. I completed the form and all the competencies, then sent it to my then manager to countersign. I was called into a meeting and asked if I really wanted to apply for this job. Of course, I said yes. I was then told, **"You have to wait until you get the tap on the shoulder,**

until then stay where you are." Why did there have to be a barrier, a challenge, a hurdle each time? I had actually started to doubt myself and had to quickly snap out of it as I knew I could do the job. I was already doing it, just without the pay. I found a way to get round my countersigning. I promise it was not illegal, and I got the job. My manager at the time was not amused at this and even more so as I got the promotion.

Thereafter, one more career progression into the role of a Deputy Director and I was asked, **"Who did you sleep with?"** You just couldn't make any of this up! This was the mentality of the people I worked with plus their own insecurities and fears. They may have been saying it as a joke, but at no point did they think that my hard work and doing well at the interview had any part to play with me getting the promotion. Really, what is wrong with people? It could have been jealousy rearing its ugly head or maybe even they genuinely thought that was how you got promoted. I think they must be getting things mixed up with the old casting couch.

I think we have now reached the point where it is now time to talk about some of the positives that came out of all those situations as sometimes we can get so caught up with everything that goes wrong that we forget the good. So where can I start?

I met some amazing individuals along the way who understood my journey and the difficulties. They took time out of their own work and found ways to help me progress. I found my own inner strength and resilience that I didn't know existed. I could have just kept my head down and bowed out gracefully but then that would not have been me. Without realising it, I had become an inspiration to many and mentored them to progress in their careers. All those years ago the furthest someone, especially female, from the BAME community, with a disability, would get to would be an Executive Officer so to go past that and more was awesome. I did that. I found MY VOICE.

In 2004 I was appointed as a Magistrate even though I was convinced I would not be successful as I was not from a well to do family, Caucasian and been educated at Oxford or Cambridge. I was proved wrong and to this day I still am a Magistrate. It was a very special day for my parents and me. This was another opportunity for me to inspire others to break down barriers and follow their dreams. To this day I still encourage and support others who have an interest in becoming a Magistrate to apply because the world is made up of different people, with different upbringings and reasons for where they are, what they do and who they become. They cannot be understood through the lens of one type of human.

2012 was a very difficult year for me, difficult not because of my position as deputy director but it was the year I faced the loss of my mum a day before her 70th birthday.

My mum was my rock and she was always in my corner, but she was here no more. Without my mum, I started to reflect on life, what I was doing and where I wanted to go. I wanted more out of life and even before I had started the journey, work stepped in to take over my life again. I had not grieved. I had gone through the motions my father had asked me to do and then I had just returned to work.

To show you just how insensitive the workplace can be, on this occasion I had notified my manager I was returning to work and arrived early in the morning to be told that I should go home as I was on the night shift. I just did not have the energy to fight. I wanted some sort of normality in life and this was it. This time of my life was pivotal in what would happen in years to come as although I had physically lost my mum, her spirit remained with me each day and watched over me, guiding me as the next phase of my journey unravelled.

Sometimes, in life things happen and at the time you just cannot comprehend what is going on or even why? Each day becomes harder to get up and do the things that would normally be easy and my day came. A big sporting event had finished and slowly people were seconded back to their departments. Others were moved on to other roles and I was asked to be part of the team that was going to close down the sporting event. This basically meant doing all the administrative work and tying up any loose ends. I never quite understood, even to this day, why I was not then put into another team and had to apply for any future roles but it was to be the start of my exit phase.

I finished the work and then was moved into another team with the manager whose focus was targets and delivery. By that, what I mean is no people's skills, no understanding of disability or illness, no caring responsibilities or any of the things that people live with and face in life. My life at work changed, but it was different this time. Was it the loss of my mum? Did the new manager push me over the edge? Was it my time to follow my dreams? It could have been any of these, all of these and some. I don't think I will ever truly know but the end of that era happened and I felt free.

It was time to gather my energies, recharge and find a path of my own. It took around a year to decide what I wanted to do. I started to write down what kind of things made me happy and the first one was talking and communicating. The list included being with people and making them happy through events. I recall being at a wedding and seeing an elderly white gentleman in a red uniform. He was making the announcements and looking after guests, the couple and working with other suppliers. I remember him saying, "And now ladies and gentlemen, it's time for the 'Akhandhya SaubhagyaVati'" in a very western way.

I remember giggling and thinking to myself, oh my god that's what I want to do, he can't even pronounce the words right. Here I am, know the religion and culture, speak the language and I want to do this. The word *want* felt very different from *need*. Throughout my employed career, I had always felt I needed to do well. I needed to put my hand up and do the jobs others did not want to do. I needed to be seen and heard for the amazing person I knew I was. Why did I need to break down so many barriers and walls then still face more challenges? Things had to change.

I did some research around becoming a Toastmaster and I contacted a few organisations. One person got back to me in a timely fashion. I say that as others got back to me a long time after. It was Richard from The English Toastmasters' Association that I spoke to and it was through the association I did both my Toastmaster and Celebrant training. I think I may currently hold the record for being the shortest Toastmaster and Celebrant in the UK which is a special gift. The extra special gift I have is to make people feel tall or even taller. In case you have forgotten, I am under five foot tall

My journey has been a tough one with challenges that I should not have had to face but it has also been one of opportunity. I learnt so much more about people, their ambitions and the disastrous way they show them. One of my biggest learnings is that I am not going to be every-

Daring to follow her dreams at the age of fifty - despite setbacks, health issues and workplace bullying, Sonal, through her passion for diversity and inclusion, is inspiring others to break down barriers and open doors to show them that they too have the opportunity to be different and do what they are truly passionate about.

As a multi-passionate, Sonal was a child performer with the English National Opera and Sadlers Wells and continued to perform through her young adult years. She has been a Magistrate with NW London (since 2004), an actress (a member of Equity & Spotlight) and a singer.

As an Indian woman in her twenty+ year career with the Civil Service, Sonal learnt a great deal, but she also made sacrifices and came across much discrimination and unconscious bias. With the help and support of her husband, their dogs and close friends she used this experience to start up her own business in the events, entertainment and life skills education industry.

For Sonal, her role as a Toastmaster & Celebrant is not just about making announcements, it is about making events bespoke and successful. She believes that it is her role to listen in order to understand - not to listen to speak. She aims to always bring the right energy into the room to elevate any special event and ensure events are special, unique and memorable for the right reasons.

Sonal has been featured in magazines such as:

Sovereign (a Global Magazine for Executives & Leading Entrepreneurs)

Khush Magazine (Asian Weddings)

WOW, Digital Magazine

Spotlight Feature in Asian Voice (newspaper targeted at British Asians)

The Metro for the Magistrate recruitment campaign

Harrow Times for her recognition at the She Awards

The Asian Wedding Directory as a Lady Toastmaster & Ceremonies Celebrant

The London Wedding Magazine as a Lady Toastmaster, Ceremonies Celebrant and Editorial

Mail Online for a story on changing careers after the age of fifty

Mail on Sunday for a story on dogs and DNA

Harrow Times for winning The Entrepreneur Award at The Women of The World Awards (WOW)

Sonal has won:

The Innovation and Excellence Awards as Best Luxury Wedding Celebrant 2020

The WOW Awards for Entrepreneur of the year 2019

The Global Wedding Awards as Best Luxury Wedding Celebrant 2019 -UK,

The BrideBook Award for Celebrant of the year 2019,

The She Awards Highly Commendable Inspirational Role Model in 2019,

The She Awards Honorary Award in 2019,

The British Asian Wedding Awards Finalist as Specialist Asian Wedding Supplier 2019

The She Inspires Award Finalist as The Best Entrepreneur 2019,

The Wedding Industry Awards Regional Finalist in the Celebrant category 2019

The MTM Awards Finalist in the National Positive Role Model 2018,

The Wedding Industry Awards Regional Finalist in the Special Touch 2018.

Sonal is a keen supporter of charity work and has been a member of Shishukunj since childhood where she previously sat on the Executive Committee. She also supports SKSN, a school in Jodhpur, India for children with polio. Sonal has been acknowledged by Barnet Council for her voluntary and charity work.

"A beautiful face will age, and a perfect body will change, but a beautiful soul will always be a beautiful soul."

CONTACT:

Website - https://www.sonaldave.com

facebook.com/sonal.dave.94

twitter.com/sonaldave68

instagram.com/sonaldave68

linkedin.com/in/sonaldave68

youtube.com/sonaldave68

pinterest.com/sonaldave68

ACKNOWLEDGEMENTS

To Abigail Horne and the team at Authors&Co for all of your support and love throughout the RSLU process, we love working with you, you ROCK.

To all our experts and speakers who have supported our Rockstars —Deep Bajwa, Sam Bearfoot, Jessica Cunningham, Margarida Kanu, Yvonne Phillip, Jo Swann, Kubi Springer and Shari Teigman

To our families who support us and cheer us on in our work, we love you and we're so grateful for you.

To all of our Rockstars, working with you has been an utter joy and we are so excited to see all the amazing things you are going to go on to achieve!